THE LUCK
OF THE DEVIL

THE LUCK OF THE DEVIL

Flying Swordfish in World War Two

Robert Le Page

Edited and introduced by
Jonathan Falla

First published in Great Britain in 2011 by
Pen and Sword Aviation
An imprint of
Pen and Sword Books Ltd
47 Church Street
Barnsley
South Yorkshire
S70 2AS

ISBN 978 1 84884 544 2

Printed and bound by CPI UK

Pen and Sword Books Ltd incorporates the imprints of Pen and Sword
Aviation, Pen and Sword Maritime, Pen and Sword Military,
Wharncliffe Local History, Pen and Sword Select, Pen and Sword
Military Classics and Leo Cooper.

For a complete list of Pen and Sword titles please contact
PEN AND SWORD BOOKS LIMITED
47 Church Street, Barnsley, South Yorkshire, S70 2AS, England
E-mail: enquiries@pen-and-sword.co.uk
Website: www.pen-and-sword.co.uk

Contents

Introduction

by
Jonathan Falla

Robert Le Page, my father, grew up on a housing estate in south-east London, the son of a window cleaner. He ended his career as a distinguished professor of sociolinguistics, respected as one of the early pioneers in the study of creole languages and multi-lingual societies. Between the very different worlds of his childhood and his scholarship, there came an experience that was profound and life-changing: his years (1941–5) with the Fleet Air Arm, flying Swordfish in the Battle of the Atlantic and with the Arctic convoys.

He wrote his memoir of the war aged eighty, in the last years of his life (he died in 2006), having a small number of copies printed for distribution to friends and family. Never mind all the distinctions he had achieved in his career in Jamaica, Malaya, the Americas, at Singapore and at York University; never mind the numerous publications, the honorary degree, the tree-lined college court named in his honour: his Fleet Air Arm days still haunted him.

After his death, I wondered if the memoir might not find a wider audience. When I came to edit it, I found that there were errors and gaps, but also that these could be filled from other sources: from a number of letters he had written to me over the years; from passages in his later academic autobiography; from many hours of conversation I had had with him over the course of four decades; and from the recollections of his wife, Gina. In 1991, the surviving 1940s aircrew of 816 Squadron held a reunion, and a booklet was put together including Robert's poems about the squadron, and various other items, in particular brief accounts by Don Ridgway and Brian Bennett, some parts of which Robert then inserted with permission into *Luck of the Devil*.

By foraging among these various sources, I was able to fill the lacunae and to add some extra information to clarify contexts. So, for example, the memoir mentions that, flying their Swordfish from

Thorney Island on the south coast to Macrihanish on the Mull of Kintyre, the squadron fell in with a wild party held at an airbase somewhere halfway – but Robert gives no more detail. However, in July 1998 I was working on a novel of my own, in part concerning Polish aircrew in wartime Britain, and I asked Robert if he had encountered any. The story of the party and the painful Polish New Year greeting (p.76) is contained in the letter I received in reply.

Other episodes are more problematic, and clearly there are questions of recall. Some memoirs of the Second World War often give an impression of crystal-clear recollection right down to details of conversation. There is a common perception that very elderly people who can scarcely remember what they had for breakfast will nonetheless display a perfect clarity regarding events seventy years ago. How correct are such memories, in truth? Often it is impossible to know; the vividness of a story is no guarantee of its accuracy.

A curious example of this occurs in Chapter One, in which Robert speaks of working on a financial audit for the Saunders-Roe Company at Cowes in 1939, and seeing there a huge flying boat under construction, the SaRo Princess. He relates the circumstances carefully, noting a colleague who was present and what had been said. But this story cannot be true: the Princess flying boat was barely even sketched out until mid-way through the war, was not ordered by BOAC until 1945, and did not make a test flight until 1952. Robert cannot have seen it in 1939, because it did not exist. There is a possibility that, immediately after the war and while waiting to go up to Oxford, he did some small audit work on Saunders-Roe for his old accountancy firm, and I thought for a moment that perhaps he was confusing a pre-war with a post-war memory. But even that is problematic, since this would have been in 1945 at the latest, when I believe little of the huge flying boat had yet been built. I considered removing the passage entirely, but I have left it in: he saw something, it made an impact upon him, and it surely contains a truth that I have not yet properly located.

Elsewhere his memories leave me negotiating with the chronology. In several conversations over the years, and also in a letter to me, he related another incident in which in the autumn of 1941 he (as observer) and his pilot were jumped by a Polish-piloted fighter aircraft while flying in a Walrus seaplane off the east coast of Scotland. Again, this is problematic. The memoir makes no mention of the incident or of any Walrus flying, and in 1941 Robert was not long into the Navy, and a long way from being a trained observer. However, I am told by Robert's FAA colleague Don Ridgway that it was quite common for observer training to include flights in a Walrus; he (Don) had done just this during his own training. So 1941 is plausible. But we have to reconcile Robert's memory with the history of both the airfields and the Polish squadrons. At the top of the letter, Robert states that the Polish fighter had come from the airfield at Crail in Fife.[1] At the bottom of the page he adds a note. He has just phoned an old squadron friend who says, no: the Poles were based at Errol, just round the corner on the Tay (an airfield I can see today from the hill behind my house, and which is used for Sunday car boot sales). But when I look at the various websites documenting Scottish Second World War airfields, and also the history of the Polish squadrons of the RAF, I find that a) Errol airfield was not opened until 1942; and b) that there was a Polish fighter squadron – 309 'Land of Czerwien' – based at Crail, but only from June to October 1942, by which time Robert was with the newly reforming 816 Squadron at Thorney Island near Portsmouth.

So, what to believe? I can hardly think that he has made the whole episode up (including the corroboration from his squadron colleague). But it doesn't seem to fit. Documents that would help resolve the issue are Robert's personal flying logbooks – but, as he relates, these are at the bottom of the sea, lost in the sinking of HMS *Dasher*. In the absence of any better solution, I have left the episode dated during his training at Arbroath, perhaps to be more fully explained another day.

For there may be other explanations. One thing I have learned while working on this memoir is that it is not only Robert's memory that is sometimes erratic, nor is it always him who is wrong. There is a doubt, for instance, over his memory of a shipbuilder's plaque (see p.75): there are a number of websites – such as the 'Fleet Air Arm Archive' – that document the history of the FAA's escort carriers, of which Robert served on four: HMS *Dasher*, *Tracker*,

Chaser, and *Empire McCabe*, and they all agree that *Dasher* was not built by the company Robert believed. If, however, I enquire as to where the *Empire McCabe* was built, most sites concur that she was built by Swan Hunter on the Tyne, but one source demurs, saying that the builder was Harland & Wolff of Belfast. Given that websites are by no means primary sources, and tend to follow each other's lead, I don't think that the outvoting of Belfast is conclusive. Somebody clearly has it wrong – and that may also be true of the information on Fife airfields and Polish squadrons.

It will be seen, then, that editing and building up a composite historical memoir like this, even of events that are just about within living memory, is a hazardous process. One meddles and corrects at one's peril. On the whole, except where there is a clear slip-up, I have not attempted to smooth out the inconsistencies or the irreconcilable; I have flagged them up in footnotes, but have let them stand.

In a few cases, there has been a passing slip of recall, easily corrected. An example is Robert's mention of Operation *Mincemeat*, the celebrated 'man who never was' deception in which the body of a fake intelligence officer was allowed to be found by the Germans, carrying documents containing vital misinformation. In the memoir, Robert says that this was part of the subterfuge associated with D-Day in 1944, but of course Operation *Mincemeat* took place in 1943, intended (successfully) to delude Hitler into believing that the Allies were about to invade Greece, not Sicily. In 2002 (after the memoir was printed), there appeared a new edition of a book[2] about the sinking of Robert's first carrier, HMS *Dasher*, in which it was claimed that the corpse used for Mincemeat was one of the drowned *Dasher* crew. I gave him a copy of the book and we discussed it at some length. He knew very well when the *Dasher* sinking had occurred; the mistake in the memoir is trivial, and I have moved the event and his reaction to our discussion to its rightful place.

*

Robert gave his memoir its present title, *Luck of the Devil*, partly because he did indeed feel lucky: there is a running theme in the memoir of his 'making good', breaking out from the confines of his poverty-struck working class London background but never forgetting them. Ending his career in some grandeur as a professor of linguistics and as the provost of one of York University's colleges, he gave the college a quintessentially Le Page motto: *The tone is low but the quality is high.*

So the war was 'a time of gifts', but sometimes of a profoundly unwanted sort.

For there was a devil in there too. He often told me that he believed his luck to have been undeserved. That, one might think, is in the nature of random luck; still, Robert looked at what had happened to his friends – drowned, or shot down, or burned, or burned out at war's end – and he could not fully understand why he had survived. So in the memoir he clings to those aspects of his own performance that go a little way towards a justification: his meticulous navigational skills, for example. He also feels deeply the few moments of virtue: the passage in which he goes to his dying mother's bedside shows conventional filial devotion, and is even sentimental, but for Robert it was also a crumb in the scales of fortune, earning him a little more of that tenuous luck.

A highly intelligent and sensitive man, a scholar and a poet, he was often terrified by the war, and distressed. He found the tumult of emotions, the fears and the loves that he experienced as a young man to be disturbing, and he never quite shrugged off the conflicts – military, and personal – that the following chapters make vivid.

*

Note: the text follows the convention of giving the names of ships such as HMS *Tracker* in italics, but not the names of land bases, e.g. HMS Daedalus.

The photographs are taken from Robert's personal album. All endnotes are editorial, by JF.

My thanks are due to Gina Le Page and family, to the Imperial War Museum (Duxford), to Don Ridgway, and to Associated Newspapers for permission to quote from the *Daily Sketch* articles by A.D. Divine.

Notes

1. Crail airfield is still (2010) well preserved in something like its Second World War state.
2. *The Secrets of HMS Dasher* by J & N Steele, 3rd ed. (2002). Robert commented that the book attributes certain details and events to *Dasher* that, in fact, concerned another 816 Squadron carrier, HMS *Chaser*. Unfortunately, he never specified which events.

CHAPTER ONE
Youth

I was the youngest of five children of an heroic mother, born on 8 December 1920 in a house on the Progress Estate in Well Hall, south-east London. The estate had been built to house workers at the Woolwich Arsenal, where my father had worked as a storekeeper during the First World War. Ours was called Martin Bowes Road; who Mr Bowes had been I had no idea, but the streets around ours had names of obvious provenance: Shrapnel Road, Artillery Road, Shooter's Hill. The latter was my father's favourite, a steep walk through the woods to get up a thirst, with a pub at the top outside which we all had to sit while he downed his pint and then brushed the froth off his moustache with the back of his hand. That was a sadly characteristic gesture.

William Henry Falla Le Page, my father,[1] was the son of a Guernsey man. The family were partly of Huguenot (French Calvinist) origins, refugees from violent religious persecution in Normandy; the Channel Islands are littered with our family names – Falla, Le Page, Tostevin and Patourel – many of them originating from the same small Normandy communities. In a Guernsey churchyard lies the Chevalier James Le Page, died 1780, my great-great-grandfather. His son Pierre Le Page was a seaman who in 1848 drowned on his first voyage as captain after his marriage, leaving his wife pregnant with my grandfather, Peter. In time, Peter came to London to work as a proofreader on a newspaper and to raise his own family.

As a child, my father William had spent many holidays with a rich uncle on Guernsey and had been brought up to expect that he would inherit the uncle's property. William left school at fourteen to go to sea as a midshipman on one of his uncle's ships that carried emigrants to the Antipodes. It was a troubled career; he had sailed to Australia, New Zealand and even the Antarctic, but somewhere in the south he had knocked the mate down and had jumped ship in Adelaide, a fugitive from justice. William seemed to evade the worst consequences; later he joined the Army and went out to South Africa and the Boer War, with a remount unit that broke and trained horses for Lord Kitchener's cavalry. Back in London, he married my mother and waited for his inheritance from his uncle, in the meantime working as a scene-shifter in a theatre, then at the Woolwich Arsenal, and then as a cinema projectionist. William lost this job as a result of losing his temper after a few lunchtime beers. Asked repeatedly to show the newsreel film of the funeral of King Edward VII, he became bored and irritated and ran it through at double speed, causing a fracas. Still, he stubbornly believed that he had 'expectations'. I can remember the day a letter came from a solicitor in Peter Port, Guernsey: the uncle had at last died. But, shortly before his death, he had married his housekeeper and had left almost everything to her, all except £800 and two very large and ghastly framed engravings. The crate was opened in our little living room and these two gilt-framed masterpieces were unpacked. One was called 'The Return of the Lifeboat'; the other was also some sea-faring drama. We had to live with these until a German bomb kindly disposed of them in 1940.

So the armed forces, and the sea, imposed upon our lives in erratic ways.

At the time of my birth, with the First World War ended, my father had lost his job at the Arsenal – one of a great many he lost in an improvident life. For a while he managed to scratch a living by cleaning windows and doing odd maintenance jobs for our neighbours on the estate, which by now belonged to the Royal Arsenal Cooperative Society. He spent most of the little he earned on beer at the pub.

I have two particularly striking photographs of my parents. One was taken on the day of their engagement: my mother, very pretty, beams with excited happiness, while my father regards her with manly adoration. He still has a robust, military cast to his looks. The family photograph (*plate 1*) taken by my brother in 1938 shows an affectionate group, my father by now a benign paterfamilias behind that droopy, beery moustache and substantial waistline, my mother smiling sweetly but looking careworn, and holding onto the family dog which, in shameless transference, was called Boozer. My sisters are beaming out at the world with a sunny confidence – which is touching, considering all the misfortunes the family had undergone – while I look rather thin and anxious, gazing down on my parents as if wondering what trouble might come next. There had been, and would be, plenty.

Much of the burden of providing for five children and paying the rent fell on my mother and her work as a dressmaker. Our living room always contained her black 'dolly' on which the dress currently under construction had to be fitted. She often had to work until late at night to get work finished, although ever since adolescence she had suffered from heart trouble – the aftermath of rheumatic fever. She seemed to live on aspirins. Meanwhile my brother Bill collected the charity handouts from the local church hall in a pram, running the gauntlet of jeers from other children. When Mother was unwell, I would cook the evening meal – it was usually Irish stew – running up and down the stairs for her instructions.

Our mother was a devout Christian, a regular churchgoer who insisted that we should go too. Her God sometimes showed her a harsh face. Her first son, Bert, whom she adored, died when he was fifteen; while playing rugger, he took a kick in the stomach, which caused a twist in his gut that proved inoperable and fatal. She believed that Bert's death was a punishment; apparently when she had found that she was pregnant with me, she had cried: 'Oh God, isn't four enough?' – and so (she believed) God had taken one away. A very large framed photo of Bert always hung on the wall opposite the foot of my parents' bed, so that she could gaze at it. I would go with her to plant and tidy his grave in Eltham cemetery, enjoying being sent with a little watering can to the communal tap. Eventually, she and my father were both buried with Bert in the same grave.

*

There were other consequences of the Guernsey inheritance, chiefly an ambition to better ourselves.

We were not unhappy in life. We had, for a start, delightful neighbours on the Progress Estate. On one side was Mr Cousins who drove a steam lorry for Jo Lyons the tea merchants. The lorry would stand outside the house all night hissing gently and leaving a little pile of ashes on the road by the morning. Next to him was the policeman, whose wife wore skirts far too short and tight to hide her horribly fat thighs. Across the road was the park keeper, who had been in the Army during the war and who, after a few beers at the pub, would stride down the road singing, 'I'm the only bloody hero in the road.' There was Eileen Porteous, who was supposedly rather smitten with me but who really only came to our house to eat my mother's rice pudding. There was a family of gypsies, big bosomy girls. At night we played endlessly a game called 'Release' or 'Prisoner's Base' in the yellow gaslight around the lamp post immediately outside our house.

But, nice as these people were, my mother wanted to 'get on'. Music provided another incentive. She was an accomplished pianist in the entertainment way, and she bought a piano from the Co-op, paying by instalments. My brother Bill was able to invite a few school friends to our house for musical evenings and, in return, he and sometimes my mother would go to the friends' homes – grander and more pretentious than ours. This fired their ambition further. Bill and my mother determined that we should move to a house with two reception rooms. Agents were consulted, careful calculations made, and a suitable house found near Well Hall station. The agent came to see us one evening to have the contract signed and to collect the deposit. But at this point my father began to shuffle his feet and look sheepish: he had spent the money on beer. There was a deathly hush before the agent left, furious at the waste of his time. Then the storm broke.

After this, Bill and my mother formed an alliance to run the family affairs. This was a continual balancing act of saving, dreaming, and taking steps to advance ourselves. We had a long way to climb. The Progress Estate house had three tiny bedrooms with double beds. My parents had one, my two sisters another, and me, Bill and a lodger called Fred all slept together in the third room. I slept in a concertina bed – a contraption with a folding canvas base that packed into a neat wooden box – along the foot of the double occupied by Bill and Fred. Apart from the beds there was little room for anything other than a washstand with a chamber pot underneath. The only heat came from the kitchen range. The privy was outside in the garden, and one of our jobs as children was tearing up newspaper into suitably-sized pieces to be strung up inside the door. On a cold night, my father would put an earthenware bottle half full of water into the oven, and then take this out to the privy, where he would sit with the hot bottle on his lap and the door open so that he could gaze at the stars.

Modern times were coming. The streetlights on the estate were still gas, lit each evening by a lamplighter with a bike and carrying a pole to turn the tap high above. But electric lighting was installed in the estate houses by the Co-op. We began to get advanced ideas. Fred, the lodger, had a crystal radio set that we would all get to listen to; when he moved out, Bill bought parts for building his own more sophisticated receiver, complete with two valves and its very own loudspeaker. By now, each back garden on the estate was sprouting a tall aerial pole. In 1929, when Bill was eighteen, the Government began a scheme to attract young men into the Royal Air Force to train as aircrew reservists. Bill entered as an electrical engineer,[2] in the meantime finally scraping together the £30 deposit needed for the family to move to Eltham. We were on the way up! My sister Kitty qualified as a teacher, while sister Amy found work with a city merchant, trading with Burma.

I was still at my first school – the Gordon Elementary, named after the general – and was sitting scholarship exams. This was a matter of great anxiety for the son of an aspiring family. Walking to the Gordon School each day I had to pass Deansfield Road school, and I was given to believe we were better than the Deansfield Road children. We kept our distance, except for ferocious snowball fights. But if I failed the scholarship exams there would be nothing for me but Deansfield Road until I was fourteen, and then a wretched job as a messenger boy, perhaps, hanging onto the back of a Carter Paterson van.

So: I was very determined. I achieved fame because, in the space of one week, I led a small gang of friends onto the roof of the school, dislodging a slate and letting rain in upon the girls' class – for which I was caned by the headmaster on the school hall stage – while also winning a scholarship to Christ's Hospital, the ancient charitable grammar school at Horsham. The headmaster at Gordon, Mr Crease, did not like me; at the announcement of the exam results, he kept my name till last and paused a long time before saying it, so that my friends had begun murmuring, 'Bad luck, Bob.' Then Mr Crease tried to scare me off by telling me that I would need eight pairs of shoes, which I knew that my parents could not possibly afford. My mother's response was characteristic: 'Never mind, my son, we'll manage.' Anyway, it was quite untrue; all she had to buy was one pair of house slippers and another of plimsolls.

But this – the first stage of my assault on the middle classes – meant that I had urgently to change my accent.

I worked my way through Christ's Hospital, always anxious that my friends in Martin Bowes Road might somehow make their way to Sussex and see me in my school uniform: a long blue coat, black knee breeches, and yellow woollen stockings – the echoes of a sixteenth-century charitable poor house. I did my best to study meticulously while also reading as widely as I could, for I was determined to be a literary man. But when I was about to leave at the age of sixteen, there was no chance of going to university. By now my family were desperate for money. My father, full of beer as usual, had twice fallen off his window-cleaning ladder and had broken first an arm, then a leg, after which he had little earning power left in him. My mother was having to work longer and longer hours at her dressmaking to make ends meet. So I needed a job. Rather disappointed in me, the headmaster – 'Oily' Flecker – took me up to London to be interviewed by Messrs Barton & Mayhew, a firm of chartered accountants by St Botolph's churchyard, Bishopsgate, which had connections with the school. I had never been in an office anywhere near as imposing. The senior partner, Mr L.I. Grant, looked at me sternly down the length of his nose and asked:

'What is you father's profession?'

I could hardly say that he was a window cleaner who kept falling off his ladder.

'He was in the Army, sir.'

Well, it was true, if you went back to the Boer War – and I could tell from the way he walked that Mr Grant had been in the forces himself. He seemed pleased with my answer; I could see him fitting me into a picture: son of an infantry officer, fatally wounded at Ypres…

I was ready to work hard as a junior audit clerk, but I had to look the part; my family clubbed together to buy me a suit from the Co-op, and a hat – though not the fashionable pork-pie or homburg. The clerk who had advised me that I should have a hat looked askance at what I produced, and sneered: 'Oh, you got one of those…'

Well, I had precious little money. My salary in the first year was thirty shillings a week, and none of my Christ's Hospital uniform was wearable now: I could hardly appear in the city in a medieval blue coat and stockings. I had to buy a season ticket for the morning train into Cannon Street (seven shillings and sixpence a week). Lunch most days consisted of a half pint of mild-and-bitter (fourpence), and some bread and cheese (twopence). I longed desperately to go to sleep in the afternoons.

But I was keen to succeed, to impress and to advance, and I applied myself to the skills and techniques of accountancy. For the first few weeks it seemed that I did nothing but add up columns of figures – so much so that I would wake up in the night mumbling to myself: *Twenty-one, thirty, thirty-eight…* This was called 'casting', and the old hands could cast the pound, shilling and pence columns all together. I was not in the business long enough quite to master that, although I won some small respect for being able to add a column accurately at speed. Just occasionally it was deemed that a job was too large or complex for my mortal skills: then the firm would summons a taxi, and despatch Miss Morris and her enormous 'portable comptometer'. Her quick fingers did it all; casting was going out of fashion, and I wanted to work the comptometer with Miss Morris. I had no idea that the skills and discipline I was acquiring would save my life in the air not long after.

Soon I was being regularly sent out of London to do company audits elsewhere. In 1937 and 1938 I spent the regatta week fashionably at Cowes, in the sun-drenched offices of the aircraft company Saunders-Roe, right on the water front, and lodged at their expense in a hotel immediately opposite across the water. They were building the 'Princess', new flying boats that were going to link together the outposts of the British Empire, flying up the Nile, for instance, and putting down on the river at nightfall, or to tropical harbours on the route to India and Australia. I would peer at these enormous contraptions with their lovely boat-hulls, wondering how on earth they could ever lift themselves off the sea into the air, while the rather fat senior clerk in charge of the audit agreed; he would point at a flying boat with his umbrella and say scornfully, 'That will never fly!' But, in fact, it was not weight that did for the great flying boats, but economics and the march of progress: the war resulted in the construction of concrete runways all over the world, while jet engines, radar and new avionics made it unnecessary to go about the globe in short daylight hops. None of that was dreamed of in 1938. I would gaze at the extraordinary aircraft and imagine them rising into the blue, streaming water.[3]

In the late summer of 1939, while the Germans were invading Poland, I was in paradise – in the guise of Milk Marketing Board audits. A team of four of us trundled about the country in a little red MG car, visiting creameries and matching the intake of milk from farmers to the amount of cream and cheese produced against the subsidy claimed. We went to the most delectable parts of south-west England: Devizes, Frome, Bradford-upon-Avon, everywhere having a country hotel with huge breakfasts, bowls of cream on every table, Wiltshire ham and Somerset bacon, long walks along the banks of the Kennet-Avon canal, and a seven-course dinner each night.

And in the meantime I had acquired a girlfriend, Gina, who lived some two miles from us. I was nineteen, Gina eighteen.

*

But then real war replaced phoney war. Hitler was poised to invade Britain; the *Luftwaffe* was seeking to destroy all the defences of the south coast. Churchill called for every able-bodied person to defend their homeland, and with thousands of others I joined the Local Defence Volunteers. I was issued with my 'uniform' – an armband printed with the letters LDV. This made us into an army under the terms of the Geneva Convention, and entitled us to its protection if we were rounded up by German paratroops in Eltham High Street. We were then issued with antique American .300 gauge rifles and a pouchful of .303 ammunition (which made us rather anxious about what would happen when we pulled the trigger). I was assigned to a platoon under the command of a First World War captain, and set to guard a golf course against airborne invasion forces. My nervous 'Halt! Who goes there?' was usually in response to the rush and scuttle of a hedgehog. After a few weeks our name was changed to The Home Guard, and we were issued with coarse cotton combat wear, camouflaged in shades of green and khaki.

Then our house was bombed.

We had seen the war coming, bit by bit. From our smart little semi-detached house on the steep hill at New Eltham, we had a grandstand view of the Thames. Most of the industrial activity seemed to be on the far side, to the north. We could gaze at the busy shipping traffic heading out across the world, at the coke and oil depots, and the huge gas works at Beckton. On the south bank, there was still plenty of open country between us and the Thames, but the trams and the trolley buses took us right down to the Woolwich Ferry, where you could cross for free as often as you liked on the paddle steamers; we would ride below decks, delighting to see the great pistons that drove the paddle wheels. Or we could cross the river *via* the Woolwich tunnel, taking the lift down below water level (or running down a great many stairs) before the long walk through the damp white-tiled tube, which echoed very satisfactorily as we yodelled our way to the north.

From the early autumn of 1940 we had become accustomed to trying to sleep against the familiar but threatening bbrr.mmm... brrr...mmm of fleets of twin-engined German bombers, Heinkel 111s, on their first probing attacks. When the Blitz began in earnest, that distant north bank became a prime target for the bombers. On the second night of the big night raids of 1940, I stepped out of our house on the hill to gaze across the valley and to see the north bank burning – an awe-inspiring, if rather remote sight. But the danger suddenly came much closer, and my feelings about the enemy changed.

By now, most of my family had dispersed to distant work and marriages. I was the only one at home with my parents; I was still just nineteen. I had spent my summer holiday painting all the woodwork of the outside of the house – windows, doors, everything – finishing the job triumphantly just in time for it to be destroyed. The borough council had invaded our garden and built us an Anderson shelter: interlocking loops of corrugated iron sunk three feet into a pit in the ground, the roof covered with the earth from the pit. I had constructed double-deck bunks in the shelter for my parents and neighbours, while I slept indoors on my concertina bed placed by the chimneybreast, the most solidly built part of the house.

On the third night of the Blitz proper, I lay on my camp bed listening to the raid. Just before midnight I heard the first four of a stick of five bombs come whistling down in succession, each one closer than the last. I did not hear the final bomb fall – but that was the one that hit the house next door, flattening it completely and blowing the roof off ours. I found myself lying on my camp bed staring up at the open sky and the searchlights stabbing out over the back garden. None of the falling wall or ceiling had actually hit me.

I struggled out over the heap of rubble to which the back of the house had been reduced (luckily I was fully clothed), out through the gaping hole that had been the French windows, over the heap of mud and concrete that covered my beloved goldfish pond, our garden shed and my old bike, and I stumbled down to the Anderson shelter from which my parents were calling to see if I was still alive. I couldn't get into the shelter itself; by this time my parents had been joined by two terrified old ladies, one of whom had been unable to control her bladder. Two helmeted air-raid wardens came hurrying down with torches to assess the damage. Luckily the house next door, which had taken the direct hit, had been empty.

The following days were utter confusion. I telephoned my brother in Sawbridgeworth a few hours after the bomb fell:

'Bill, have you any spare beds in your house for Mum and Dad?'

'Oh? Getting too hot for you in that house, is it?'

'Bill, we don't have a house any longer.'

My parents – both of them now increasingly frail – were shocked and shaking. Suddenly, the war meant something more than a gentlemanly fight between heroes in a foreign field: now the enemy was overhead and trying to kill my God-fearing mother and my feckless but kindly father, here in their own home in front of my eyes. I managed to get my bewildered parents with a suitcase each to the Green Line coach station and onto a bus to Hertfordshire. My brother by some miracle discovered a Quaker family anxious to rent out half of their large house to respectable city folk like us before evacuees from London's now heavily bombed east end could be billeted on them. They knew nothing of the beer and window-cleaning ladders. They got my parents, my girlfriend Gina and her mother and baby sister, while I stayed in London to salvage what I could. There in the wrecked parlour lay the last of my father's Guernsey inheritance: *The Return of the Lifeboat* and its companion-piece, with rubble punched through the middle of them and their garish gilt frames smashed to kindling. The air-raid wardens helped me find a removal man with a lorry for whatever was worth saving. I dug out my ancient and also rather shocked bicycle and moved in with my girlfriend's father.

For the next few weeks I cycled each working day from Eltham into the City. Each day I would have to make my way around fresh bomb damage, but at least on the bike I was not delayed by damaged railway lines – for the flashes from the conductor rail of the Southern Railway[4] made it an easy target for the German bomb aimers at night. At weekends I would take my decrepit bike and cycle over to Sawbridgeworth to see Gina and my family, crossing the Thames on the Woolwich Ferry, then up through Epping Forest, thirty miles or more.

*

Then my call-up papers arrived.

When I had become liable for military service, I had volunteered for the Fleet Air Arm. Maybe it was the lurid but entertaining *The*

Return of the Lifeboat, or some vague inheritance from my father's career at sea (I couldn't see myself training cavalry horses; cats were about my limit). Maybe it was the thought of the flying boats at Cowes. More likely, however, it was something much more visceral: I had a dread of confronting a German with a bayonet. I hoped that by going first to sea, and then into the air, I would never meet that fate.

So I had waited, knowing that it was coming, that there was no avoiding it, but never knowing day by day how it would actually work out for me, or when the letter would come. When, one day, the papers arrived, I went into the Barton & Mayhew office in the City and told the head clerk. A few minutes later, Mr L.I. Grant sent for me. They'd been pleased with me, he said, and would like to do something for me while I was serving. They paid my mother an allowance of ten shillings a week right through the war; they thought I was a war orphan and her sole support. Well, they were pretty much right.

Notes

1. i.e. the grandfather of the present editor, Jonathan Falla.
2. A career he followed all his life, culminating with doing the wiring of the Kariba dam hydroelectric scheme.
3. This is a puzzle, as discussed in my introduction (p.8). Robert's statement that the flying boat was the Saunders-Roe Princess (a truly monstrous double-decker) cannot be correct, as the Princess was not on the drawing board in 1938, and did not fly until 1952, the project being abandoned not long after. What he saw in 1938 could have been a Shorts Empire, one of the larger flying boats of its day; the two companies were on the cusp of a merger. Otherwise, the incident must be post-war.
4. The Southern Railway was the commuter system operating to the south and west of London, first opened in 1923 as a rival to the expanding Underground. It used a third-rail power supply.

CHAPTER TWO

Learning to Observe

HMS Daedalus was the Royal Naval Air Station at Lee-on-Solent, just across the harbour from Portsmouth. By 1941, Portsmouth harbour was a peculiar place, filled with activity, littered with defences, barrage balloons and camouflage netting, sandbagged anti-aircraft gun positions, searchlights and sirens, military policemen strutting about self-importantly, hurrying recruits like myself – always late, always slightly unsure where we were meant to be next, always being shouted at – but for all this warlike bustle there was not a great deal of shipping in the harbour, because it was, of course, far too near to enemy-held France and the *Luftwaffe* to let a capital ship sit waiting for a bomb to be dropped down its funnel. The Home Fleet, by and large, was up on the Clyde or at Scapa Flow, chasing the *Bismarck* or out escorting convoys.

There were frequent attacks by small groups of Stuka dive-bombers, which had the effect of keeping everyone's nerves a-jangle, but the truth was that for all its glorious naval traditions, for all its echoes of Nelson and the *Victory*, Portsmouth was now a significant military target only for its oil storage facilities. Otherwise, the *Luftwaffe* was far more interested in the south coast airfields and in the industries of London. Around the harbour, the fights tended to be an angry duel between the screaming Stukas and the furious (and largely impotent) machine-gunners on barrack block roofs. If nothing else, it was a useful introduction to the business of wartime existence. New boys like me flinched at every attack. Old hands nonchalantly strolled the other way.

Had I known about the dismal state of the Fleet Air Arm,[1] I might have thought better of applying for it. It was the Cinderella service *par excellence*; only in 1938 was there appointed for the first time a Sea Lord to oversee naval aviation as Chief of Naval Air Services. When I was issued with my official two-volume *Manual of Seamanship*, I noticed that it referred to the 'fleet air arm' just like that, in small letters – a note of contempt if ever there was one. Between the wars the FAA had been handed over to the RAF for what might now be called 'asset-stripping' before its return to the Navy just before the war – which is to say, there had been minimal investment in aircraft or training, while all the best aircrew seemed to have been absorbed by the RAF. The FAA was left a fraction of the size it had been in 1918. By 1939 the FAA's stock was a laughable collection of machines with which the Wright brothers would have felt at home; its most modern fighter – just brought into service at the outbreak – was the Gloster Gladiator, a 'new' biplane. There were in 1939 few Naval Air Stations, just one modern aircraft carrier (*Ark Royal*) at sea, and a total of a mere 230 planes and 350 pilots. I suppose I might have seen it – from the point of view of promoting my skills – as a seller's market.

I had requested to be trained as a pilot; I believed I had some technical ability and, after all, I had helped Bill to construct his radio set and had rigged the aerial in the garden. I knew that I was precise and careful in whatever work I was given, because Mr L.I. Grant at the accountancy firm had said so. While I had a temper at times, and was certainly furious at the Germans for what they'd done to our house (just after I'd painted it) and to my goldfish pond, I did secretly wonder whether I was entirely capable of the cold killing aggression that being an attack pilot might demand. I had never been up in an aeroplane: few people had, in 1941. The little I knew of aviation consisted of the ungainly flying boats at Cowes, and the Blitz, in which I had witnessed aircraft trying to destroy the city of London and kill its inhabitants, and another lot of aircraft trying to kill the first lot. I had seen planes destroyed – which implied the agonizingly painful death of their occupants. That was pretty much all that flying meant to me.

On the other hand, there was that family trait: the urge to better ourselves, strong in me. A Fleet Air Arm pilot: that was the thing to be – professional and skilled and a tad glamorous too. But just now I was anything but glamorous; I was a Naval Airman 2nd Class, and you didn't get many lower forms of life.

Here in Portsmouth, for two weeks we felt sorry for ourselves, slightly feverish and with aching arms from endless inoculations and vaccinations. We were issued with our uniforms, tried not to feel ridiculous in bell-bottomed trousers, and learned how to dhobi (that curious Indian term that had slipped into the Navy) our blue denim collars so that none of the blue dye ran into the white stripes. And we were issued with our pocket edition of the Gospel of St John – 'indicating The Way of Salvation by Emphasised Passages' – with its solemn message from the King:

> To all serving in my Forces by sea or land, or in the air, and indeed, to all my people engaged in the defence of the Realm, I commend the reading of this book. For centuries, the Bible has been a wholesome and strengthening influence in our national life, and it behoves us in these momentous days to turn with renewed faith to this Divine source of comfort and inspiration.
> September 15, 1939.

I'm not sure that faith was my first thought at the time – we were so frantically busy! – but my mother's God-fearing influence was profound, and the rich rolling language of the Authorised Version had been part of the making of the nascent literary man in me. It said in the booklet: 'What the compass and instruments are to the naval officer and the ordnance map is to the field officer, so the Bible is to us in our journey through life.' I have that tiny but wholesome and strengthening Gospel to this day, tucked inside my code books – which seems rather appropriate: one lot of urgent messages inside another.

More and more we learned. We might aspire to fly, but we were not to forget where our loyalties lay. Just in case we *did* forget, at our initial training station at Lee-on-Solent there was a large model of a fully rigged ship with the legend underneath: 'Join the Fleet Air Arm – but be a sailor first.'

Hence the copies of the *Manual of Seamanship* that we all received, with its detailed directions as to how to be a sailor. Its very first instruction – even before the matter of saluting – covered the manner in which a sailor makes up his hammock in the prescribed fashion. To begin with, the very language was remote:

> The bight of the lanyard is placed over the hammock hook

and the end rove through the ring, the hammock is then triced up to the height required, and the end secured with a double or single sheet bend.

Bight of the which? Rove and triced? What did any of this mean to a junior accountant's clerk from Eltham? The only sheets I knew were on my concertina bed at my parents' house in Progress Road, and were not bent. I thought of that little bedroom, and my brother and Fred the lodger sharing the big bed. We would never have passed muster. At Daedalus we slept in bunk beds; I had an upper bunk, which I was glad about, since the lad who had the bunk beneath me had the unhappy habit of not getting out of bed to empty his bladder when he'd gone off to sleep with a lot of beer in him.

There was in the *Manual of Seamanship* a chart of how we should lay our equipment out on our hammocks for inspection: our *socks or stockings* and *drawers* and our *black silk handkfs* (sic). Then there was our *sun helmet and cover (foreign stations only)*, and, of course, our *duck jumpers* (our what?). Was this really war?

We learned how to salute with the palm flat downwards like proper sailors – however much we might itch to be airmen. We struggled to learn the subtleties of rank and the infinite little ways in which these are marked in the Navy, including the important fashion hint that 'subordinate officers do not wear lace', and the sad news that 'the rating of Captain of Gun is being allowed to die out'. We learned to tie knots – again, in the Navy fashion, still no hint of Air Force style. We learned the difference between a joggle shackle and a jigger, and how to put a tail on the latter. We learned all the bits of warships; long before we boarded one, we were supposed to know what all the bits were called.

We learned gems of naval folklore, mostly about Nelson; we learned to sing:

When I am a civvy, and wear a civvy suit,
I'll walk into Trafalgar Square and give Nelson this salute:
Shove off, get stuffed, you stupid fucking bastard!

A bit of crude bravado to show that (at the end of two weeks in which we had not yet been to sea) we were seasoned mariners.

Next, we had to learn how to shoot. We were hurried away to HMS *Excellent*, the naval gunnery school at Whale Island, a much-feared establishment where everything had to be done at the double, and where if you dawdled or hesitated an NCO would stalk up behind and screech at you. There we were presented with every sort of firearm we might find on a ship: cannon, pistols and rifles, even machine guns – there was nothing quite like the noise and violent thrashing of a machine gun in one's hands for making one realize that this really was a war, and I thought again of that German coming at me with a bayonet. Then there were all the aircraft's offensive weapons: the bombs, the rockets, the depth charges and torpedoes. We took things apart and put them together again, while I wondered vaguely (but would not have dared ask) under what circumstances a pilot would want to reassemble a torpedo in mid-air.

But this was the Navy, and we must also learn to rush up and down the tarmac with a six-inch shell in our arms, ram it into the breech of a gun (hoping not to get the tips of our fingers nipped as the breech door slammed shut), and make-believe we were sinking the *Bismarck* or whatever enemy might get in our way. Then we would do it on a real ship's deck – but at anchor – trying not to trip up over every welded deck-seam as we ran, then to take aim at some destroyer or corvette in the harbour and call it the *Tirpitz*. In the meantime, the Fire Discipline Signals were pounded into us:

Signal PK : 'No enemy ship is to be left unfired at.'

I wondered how you checked on that, imagining the Admiral sending puzzled enquiries round the Fleet: *So, now then: who's firing at what?*

Signal PC : 'Concentrate fire on leading ships of column.'

Did ships still fight in columns? It seemed curiously Napoleonic. Some of the instructions sounded comic and arcane; one could only guess at their meaning:

'The Admiral may indicate that it is not his policy to employ an umbrella barrage.'

A barrage of umbrellas: something you might employ against the

Stuka dive-bombers, a tactic at least demonstrating proper sangfroid.

To begin with I didn't worry overmuch about learning all these: I thought I might pick and chose intelligently, as I had done with the best literature I had met with at Christ's Hospital, and I cheerfully believed that, as the pilot I intended to be, I'd have no pressing use for deck gunnery signals. This was an error. HMS *Excellent* thought otherwise: we were drilled and tested and tested again and I soon learned that the Navy was not interested in my arrogant notions of useful and less-useful knowledge. I began to hear how many men were 'dipped' from flying training – that is, were dropped, for not having the qualities of an officer, or for being technically not up to it, or for not knowing the proper use of the admiral's umbrellas. Once dipped, those men would find themselves below decks as an ordinary seaman, with the humiliation of having aspired to something better and failed. I was determined not to fail, but was already scared that my background would show, that the beer-and-ladders would out, that my accent would give me away. I resolved that, if nothing else, my knowledge of codes and calculations would be faultless, and I began to thank my time in accountancy for the discipline.

But there were so many codes to be learned. Every day we spent half-an-hour sharpening our knowledge of Morse, and how to transmit it. (It's a skill that, once acquired, you don't lose; in the 1950s coming back from work in Jamaica to London on a banana freighter, I was happy to keep a few watches for the radio officer.) There were plenty of other codes too: the Inter-Service Pyrotechnic Signals Code, for instance:

> Red pyrotechnic signals of any type, at sea: ship or aircraft in distress.
> Two red Very lights, by Aircraft Carrier (day only): no landing.

I would speculate on a dozen appalling scenarios for such signals: the carrier with fires raging on its flight deck, or starting to list and then to sink, the helpless aircraft fluttering about overhead, with nowhere to land and only empty miles of water…

Succession of white Very lights : Emergency landing. Am
compelled to land due to engine or other trouble.

What other trouble? I saw myself in a flaming cockpit, trying to
wrestle a wallowing aircraft into some sort of approach run, and
meanwhile frantically trying to recall how many of my white Very
lights constituted 'a succession'. And how would I remember the
difference between:

Green Very Light or Green Rocket (accompanied by 8s in
Morse by flashing or sound): from Examination Service,
signal to Examination Battery: hostile action on part of
incoming vessel.

And:

Succession of Orange or White lights fired by Mortar, Rocket
or Very Light Pistol: local recall.

What was an examination service? What if I needed an orange
rocket but could only find a green one in the box? I trembled at the
confusion I might cause in the entire fleet if I got it wrong, and again
resolved to put my meticulous learning habits to work. There was
one signal that made me think ahead to the convoys I had heard of,
and to what I had let myself in for. It was a signal used by Naval
aircraft:

Series of white smoke puffs at sea: I am flying along the
track in the wake of enemy torpedoes.

I visualized myself in my aircraft tracking a torpedo that was
heading straight for my own aircraft carrier. What if they couldn't
see me and my white puffs? Could I catch their attention by
waggling my wings? What if the bloody fools weren't watching?

Having requested that glamorous pilot training, I was sent for
another medical, which included my teeth. I concluded that this
was part of the glamour: as a pilot, one had to look good. There was
also a more thorough eye test. The doctor said nothing at the time,
indeed hardly looked at me, but scribbled on his forms and called
for the next candidate. I returned to my unit cheerfully enough,
wondering how long I'd have to wait. It wasn't long. The
Commanding Officer summoned me.

I wasn't fit to be a pilot. I stared at him in incomprehension.

'It's your eyes,' he said. 'I'm sorry, but there's something odd about them. The optometrists say that you'd be unable to judge heights. You'd always be cutting the engine twenty feet above the deck or something.'

I could do nothing but mumble my disappointment.

'Look, Le Page, I'm putting you down for observer training. It's flying, it's skilled work, you've got the brains for it, and they're short of people.'

Perhaps my supposedly wonky eyes meant that I'd see *Bismarck* floating twenty feet above the water. But I held my peace. I'd no desire to be dipped.

In the coming days people did their utmost to persuade me that I should consider myself honoured. Who'd want to be a pilot? Pilots were just drivers, mere chauffeurs. Observers were the intellectual cream of the Navy (so it was forcibly said); indeed, there were stories of men who had volunteered for observer training and who, after a while of not doing so very well, had been told that they were 'mentally deficient' and had been transferred to pilot training where their limited reasoning capacities might be sufficient. Observers told the pilot where to go, what to do when he got there, and how to get back again. More than that: observers would tell the admiral below where his enemy was, and what that enemy was up to. Without a good air observer, the admiral could only take educated guesses as to the movements of the opposition. Without a good observer, a pilot might wander forlornly about the sea until he ran out of fuel. Or he'd bomb the *Prince of Wales* instead of the *Tirpitz* because he was too excited – or just too unobservant – to tell the difference. (We didn't yet know that a flight of Swordfish, complete with their sharp-eyed and astute observers and supposedly hunting the *Bismarck*, had attacked and almost sunk our own *Sheffield* by mistake. It could have been me.)

And we would not just be map-readers. If the aircraft carried no air gunner, then the observer had to do the gunnery and the radio too, and take the photographs, and also had to cope with the cutting-edge technology – the ASV, or 'air-to-surface vessel' radar, still in its infancy and tricky to handle.

"Didn't you say you'd helped your brother build a radio? There you go, then, you're the chap with the brains for this."

Be proud, they said again and again: be proud! Actually, there was another reason for all this build-up of observers: the FAA was (as the CO had suggested) terribly short of them. This was not because a particularly high degree of intelligence was required; it was because a ship carrying a group of trainees *en route* for Trinidad for an intensive course had been torpedoed in mid-Atlantic.[2]

*

I never got to Trinidad either. My observer training took place in a smaller, colder world: the Royal Naval Air Station at Arbroath, on the east coast of Scotland. There were brief interludes at the Signals School at Eastleigh, back at the Gunnery School at Whale Island, and one or two other intellectual centres of excellence, but Arbroath was the heart of the matter. It took ten months, in which time the war seemed to march on without me.

At Arbroath, having mastered seamanship, we now studied airmanship – for we still hovered uncertainly between air and water. Truly, the notion of an FAA was still new enough to cause confusion in the minds of Their Lordships, and there came a signal from the Admiralty that passed into legend. It concerned knots: 'In future, aircraft will be secured in an airmanlike rather than a seamanlike manner.'

We studied meteorology; we studied air gunnery; it was put to us in the politest euphemisms that although we as observant intellectuals would not normally be expected to shoot back at enemy aircraft coming at us from astern spitting flame, there might nonetheless be circumstances in which our TAG (telegraphist air gunner) would be unable to undertake that duty. He might be absent, or indisposed, or dead. In which case we should, if possible, grab the single machine gun and fight for our lives.

We did interminable drill – and here I had a slight head start as we'd been through all that in the Officer Training Corps at Christ's Hospital (one of the few times we'd been allowed to take off the long blue coats and woollen stockings). We studied radio; we studied signals and yet more signals: semaphore, Morse again, coloured flags...

After a while, a certain pride really did develop. Yes, we were observers, the watchful intelligence of the Navy, capable of navigating with a high degree of accuracy and of relaying to the fleet vital knowledge of the enemy's manoeuvres (once we'd got the hang of all the codes). We were officer-cadets, with white bands round our naval caps instead of a ship's name, making us immediate targets for the disciplinary fury of petty officers and chief petty officers until we were commissioned. But in due course we would be lieutenants, or better; there were squadrons where the Commanding Officer was not a pilot but an observer.

But there were limits to our grandeur: we were certainly not pukka-RN. Had I joined the Navy – in line, of course, with my father's glorious career knocking the mate down on that emigrant ship to Australia – I might have trained as an RN observer with real RN status, since up until 1939 things had been organized in a very convoluted manner: observers had been officers of the regular Royal Navy, and part of the company of a ship. Indeed, it wasn't until c.1941 that observers received any sort of flying badge or wings for the uniform; who, after all, would want such a demeaning badge, if you were a Navy man? Aircraft were allocated to the ship along with their pilots (just drivers, you recall), and would obediently carry the officer aloft to make his observations. In due course the squadron might well move on, but the naval officer-observer would remain with his ship until the next aircraft (plus driver) turned up.

But now it was decided that we observers should stick with our aircraft. This might seem to make obvious practical sense: the pilot and observer would learn to work as a team, and learn also to trust each other's judgement. As I came to understand, pilots put their lives in the hands of the observers quite as much as *vice versa*, since an aircraft that got lost was, frequently, lost.

There were counter arguments, however: the Admiral would want to trust his observers, on whom all his battle tactics might depend, and surely the way to achieve that was to have the man part of the regular ship's company. To me – with that aspiration to

34

'get on' always present – the notion of a regular place in the flagship's wardroom was seductive.

But no: observers would now not only be regular aircrew: we would be part of a *squadron*. We were commissioned into the Air Branch of the Royal Naval Volunteer Reserve; this made us 'Wavy Navy'. By the time I joined, the badge insult had been resolved: the gold-braided stripes on our sleeves were to have a fetching wavy wobble in it, with an additional 'A', while as an observer I would have the wings of an angel on my left sleeve above the curling golden waves. These wings were attached to a round 'O'; one wing pointed heavenward. But – lest we forgot our loyalties – the 'O' contained an anchor. Pilots had an anchor too, but their wings were flat. Just drivers.

*

It was at Arbroath that we began to fly; there we met for the first time aircraft that we could actually climb into – as opposed to admiring flying boats across the water at Cowes, or glowering at them over the skies of London and Portsmouth. It is difficult today to imagine how new aircraft still seemed to us. The planes with which the FAA was equipped were not antediluvian to a young man who had never flown at all. To us, all aircraft were a thrill and a novelty. I'm not sure that, when volunteering for the FAA, it had really occurred to me to speculate as to what sort of aircraft the Fleet possessed. Possibly I had dreamed that the great cruisers went into battle towing a wallowing flying boat in their wake.

The first training aircraft we encountered was the Blackburn Shark. This was an open cockpit biplane with very few qualities and not a single modern aspect to its design, notwithstanding the fact that it had only been in service with the FAA for some ten years. It had, perhaps, the virtue of being very slow: in a Blackburn Shark nothing happened very quickly, so that generally one could work out what should have happened.

So, now I got into the air. Aircraft construction – at least, the sort the FAA got – was extraordinarily basic: a framework over which was stretched canvas painted with dope to make it stiff and tight. I remember tapping on the fuselage slightly incredulously, as I lowered myself for the first time onto the wooden floorboards hoping that I wouldn't put a foot through the bottom – like missing one's step in a house loft and sticking a shoe through the plaster ceiling. My *Manual of Seamanship* (in which there were a few disdainful pages about floatplanes) advised that one should tread very circumspectly on aircraft:

> Most aircraft consist of a light metal or wood framework covered with doped linen fabric, and if it is necessary to walk or sit on the machine, great care must be taken that the weight is placed on some suitable portion of the structure. Men working on aircraft should invariably wear rubber soled shoes…

As in the Yeats' poem: *Tread lightly, because you tread on my dreams.*

There was another training aircraft for us: the Percival Proctor. This was used almost entirely for tuition in radio and other communications, but, compared with the Shark, it looked positively go-ahead – and had indeed been derived from something called a Vega Gull, which had on occasion been used for racing. True, it had a fixed undercarriage, but its wooden frame was covered in metal sheeting and the wheels crouched in rather elegant little pods. Above all, it had an enclosed cockpit, which made shouting at students easier. We could be taken up two by two in the Proctors, together with the pilot and an instructor, and trained in radio work.

And at last, we met the Swordfish.

This remarkable aircraft belonged, like the Blackburn Shark, to the age of Biggles – yet like the Shark it had been designed less than a decade before. The Swordfish looked much like an improved Shark. Again, it was a biplane; it had a superabundance of wires holding its fabric wings together, hence its universal name of 'Stringbag'. There are those who claim that the origin of the name was not the wires, but referred to the plane's capacity to carry almost anything you cared to stuff in or onto it. Such people have never read poetry, or listened to the scansion of that fine old FAA song:

> Bring back, bring back,
> Oh bring back my Stringbag to me, to me…

–in which the stress in the line falls clearly on the 'string' and not on the 'bag', as it would do if we were talking about shopping. Or so I told myself, in my literary moments. Like most things in language, the truth is uncertain and probably a bit of everything. Certainly the Swordfish could carry almost anything you asked.

The airframe was largely metal, canvas covered and so simple in construction that a skilled crew of fitters could cannibalize several wrecked aircraft on a carrier, and put together something that flew. And flew it did; a more stolid and solidly reliable aircraft was never built, its liking for the air making it uniquely qualified for that Second World War slang term for all aircraft: a 'kite'. Like the box kite of metal spars and cotton cloth I'd once flown with my brother Bill above New Eltham hill, the Swordfish took to the air and liked to stay there.

It was a large machine: the wingspan was forty-five feet, the fuselage thirty-six feet long. But in spite of its size and its 690-horsepower engine, even on a good day with a following breeze it could barely haul itself through the air at 130 mph. All those wings and wires and the fixed undercarriage got caught in the air dreadfully. Put it into a steep dive and still the airspeed indicator seldom flickered above 200 miles an hour. This absurd speed had advantages: attacking fighter aircraft almost invariably over-shot the Swordfish, which would turn sedately and flap away in another direction. If fired on from the beam, the speed defied all common sense; German fighter or flak crews would shoot well in front of the aircraft, expecting the aircraft to fly into the fire – but the Swordfish would always be late for the rendezvous. This was as well, since we had just one forward-firing machine gun, which would hardly trouble a German fighter, while the rear air gunner standing in his canvas cockpit with his single Vickers gun was hardly fearsome. On convoy protection patrols, especially in the mid-Atlantic where shore-based enemy aircraft could not reach us, we sometimes did without the air gunner altogether, replacing him with an extra fuel tank. On the rare occasions where shooting was required (at a surfaced submarine, for instance), we observers might do that too, juggling that duty with operating the radio and keeping track of the navigation.

The low speed was in certain respects a huge advantage at sea. When it came to landing on an aircraft carrier – the ship heading into wind but steaming away from you – by the time you cut the engine over the deck, the Swordfish could be moving at barely 10 miles per hour relative to the deck, making it easy for both the arrestor wires and the handling crew to grab it. But there was a downside: if you were flying astern of the fleet and the wind was strong, you might be hard pushed to catch up. (When later we were flying over the North Atlantic convoys, that could be an uncomfortable position; a Swordfish delayed when the wind picked up might never be seen again.)

Even climbing into a Swordfish was a performance. There was a little ladder jutting below the fuselage on the port side (like horses, one boards aircraft from the left), and above that a series of toeholds that one ascended as though rock-climbing; if you started out with the wrong foot, the manoeuvre was impossible. Starting the motor was an even more primitive procedure. There was just the one engine – on the Swordfish, a nine-cylinder radial Bristol Pegasus, or 'Peggy' – but this was heavy to turn. The procedure was this: one stood on the undercarriage on the port side, inserted a crank handle into a hole and began winding up an inertia flywheel. Meanwhile, just above you, the pilot would be fiddling with his throttle and fuel mixture taps. When the flywheel was spinning nicely, you shouted 'Contact!' – at which the pilot pulled the starter wire so that the engine, the flywheel and the propeller locked. There would be coughs and splutters of blue smoke – and with luck, Peggy sprang to life. She usually did, even in the Arctic.

This was not normally the work of elite intellectuals such as observers; it was the job of ground crew. But everyone, observers and air gunners too, was trained to do it also, in case we landed in an alien place where Peggy's ways were not known, or there was simply no one to help.

The Swordfish had been originally designed for the Greek navy, while the Blackburn Shark was purchased by the Portuguese. Was that why both had open cockpits? It might have been rather delightful to drift slowly above the Mediterranean or the Algarve in an open cockpit, but I never had that pleasure; in the Arctic, the cockpits had fewer charms. They were unheated, of course. Here the pilot had an advantage, for he had some small warmth from the back of the engine. The air gunner and I had nothing. So, we learned to wrap up well. In training we were equipped with nothing more than our standard uniforms with a windproof gabardine Sidcot suit over, but the training schools were still in part run by RAF personnel, and we were sometimes able to cadge leather, fur-lined flying jackets. When winter came, we rapidly learned the value of silk underwear.

*

At Arbroath we were introduced to all these bewildering problems, and to the chaos and confusion and cramped conditions in a cockpit, on our first few 'familiarization' flights. My first flight was in daylight, of course. I leant against the canvas-and-metal-strutted side of the aircraft, astonished yet again at the primitive construction; fighter aircraft, I knew, had armour plating built into the back of the pilot's seat, so that at least he would not get bullets in his spinal cord. I had canvas to protect me. Perhaps, if attacked, one could lie down inside the Swordfish and hide.

We were taken up in Sharks and Swordfish one by one, and wafted sedately over Arbroath and out to sea, learning for the first time what the earth looks like from above, and how the colour of the sea changes as it deepens. Arbroath is a small town even today; in 1941 the airfield covered much the same area as the burgh. I photographed it from the air; I was trained in photography, for taking snaps of German pocket battleships at anchor. On those first flights I gazed through my goggles down into the backyards of the fishing population, and I tried taking bearings on the compass. Hunkered down on the little folding leather stool, I'd try fiddling with the radio, of which the receiving speakers were part of my flying helmet. I had a small head-start there also, the result of spending so many hours in the infinitely delicate art of tuning our radio at my parents' home. I practised sending interminable Morse messages down to the airfield below (discovering that this is rather harder when wearing leather flying gloves), or attempted to tune the crystal radio by the absurdly crude means of dangling more or less aerial wire (weighted with little lead balls) beneath the aircraft; not even Fred the lodger's crystal set in south London had been quite that rudimentary. I would peer down into the radar tube (the very latest equipment – perhaps the one thing in which we were actually 'modern') hoping I wouldn't be required to fix it in mid-flight, with my supposed facility for radio. And I would experiment with my rubber speaking-tube, which connected me to the pilot (like an oversized stethoscope, attached over my ears). To attract the pilot's attention, the observer would stand up in his cockpit and lean forwards to punch the pilot on the head; the latter would then pay attention to his end of the tube. This system was functional unless (as could happen) the observer had muddled his speaking tube with his pee-tube, in which case there would be bubbling noises and a great deal of shouting. Speaking with the air gunner behind me was just a matter of waving our arms and yelling.

Navigation, though: that was the heart of the training. We learned to reconcile a map with whatever one could see a thousand feet below, while not letting the map be whipped out of the cockpit by the breeze. We each developed our own personal techniques for using a chartboard in the open but cramped cockpit, either squatting on the small folding stool and balancing the board on our knees, or hanging the board from the bulkhead, which was the back of the pilot's cockpit ahead of us. If we did that, a problem arose: where on earth to put our parachutes? They were supposed to be slung from that same bulkhead, held in position by thick rubber bungees.

Our studies never let up – and most critical of all was the art of dead reckoning navigation. By this, we would live or die. If we got our calculations wrong, our Swordfish, with our pilots and gunners, would be lost in every sense, circling vainly and searching for some glimpse of ships or land until our fuel ran out. However brave and skilful our pilots, if the dead reckoning was wrong, we were all finished. So, in these classes, I paid attention.

It might not seem so complex in theory: you have a course to fly to find your airfield or carrier, you know where you are starting from, you have a chart, dividers and a compass – these are calculations that anyone could master. But what if it's dark, and you have nothing but a handheld torch? What if you have nothing better than your own knees to balance the chartboard on? What if the turbulence threatens to hoik your chart out over the side of the aircraft? What if you're exhausted by long cold hours in your noisy open cockpit? What if it's raining?

For dead reckoning to work, you have to know pretty exactly how fast you are flying over the surface, and in order to do that you must know not only your own speed through the air but the wind speed and direction also. Given that the Swordfish was flying at only 70 or 80 knots, small differences in wind speed made that much more of a difference to accuracy. We could know our own speed through the air thanks to the pitot tube, a simple enough device in which the air passing over the wing pushes against a column of fluid. Even modern jets use something similar, although on a modern jet, there are probably so many GPS instruments that you'd hardly need to know anyway; the computers doubtless make allowances and work it all out for you.

But the speed at which the wind carried us over the surface of the earth was more problematic. Over land, you can take two established landmarks and record your flying time over the distance between them. You cannot do that above the monotonous sea. So, a ridiculous procedure had been worked out: we dropped things over the side.

In daylight, this 'finding a wind' was not too difficult. Over the sea, I was trained to lean out of my cockpit and drop a small smoke float, clicking a stopwatch and yelling 'Turn!' into the rubber speaking-tube. The pilot would swing right round 180 degrees, flying straight back on our tracks. When ninety seconds had passed, I would yell again into the tube – 'Turn!' – and the pilot would swing us back round onto our original course. I'd take careful note of how long it took us to get back to the position of the smoke float, and by means of a few swift sums I would know how strongly the wind was blowing and (from the smoke) which way. Again, the value of punctilious accountancy training: the thought of getting these calculations wrong – and the consequences – were terrifying, and my studies were meticulous to the point of obsession. On convoy air-cover duty – when you needed to know not only where you were, but, above all, how long it would take you to catch up with the carrier – we would go through this every half hour at least, especially if you were flying in the unpopular position astern of the convoy.

Everything could go wrong, of course, if it was too dark or the weather too bad for me to be able to see a thing, or because we were in a warlike hurry and couldn't take time out to drop smoke flares. Then all I could do was take an educated guess at our speed over the earth. Above a desert, this might be especially awkward, if there was nothing significant to see. Even over European fields, ground visibility could be awkward and deceptive; it is sometimes fondly imagined that from the air everything below is laid out like a nice clear map, but in reality you spend half your time puzzling over details that don't seem to quite correspond to the details on your chart (and was that the Edsel road we just crossed, or the back road to Kirriemuir…?) And what if a fog comes in? Or that clinging Scottish sea-mist, the 'haa', wafting in over land and obscuring everything?[3]

You had to believe fervently in your sums and the last check you'd taken on the wind, which might have been a while ago unless, of course, you could see the surface of the sea beneath you, in which case you were expected to be able to estimate the approximate speed of the wind by the shape and size of the waves.

Day by day – for some ten months – we practised our navigation, while our pilots learned how to fly in close formation over the tops of the waves as though engaged in a torpedo attack on an enemy cruiser. We began to get used to the idea of the pilot's total reliance on our calculations, learning to give clear instructions before the nervous pilot yelled 'Which way?' down the speaking-tube. We memorized the formulae, and got used to the Swordfish and all the skills – at once so primitive and so precise – required to stay alive in her. In the meantime, we came to regard her with respect, and not only for her flying qualities For was it not torpedoes from carrier-born Swordfish that, just months before, had stopped the *Bismarck*, wrecking her steering and sending her helplessly back into mid-Atlantic to be destroyed by the Royal Navy? Was it not Swordfish that had sunk the pride of the Italian navy at Taranto?

The ungainly old bat could do remarkable things. One felt better in the open cockpit, remembering this.

Arbroath, however, was home not only to the No. 2 Observer School but also the Deck Landing School. This had just one educational facility: out of the large cross of black tarmac runway, one part was constructed of a pale concrete and was marked out to look like the deck of an aircraft carrier.[4] It was fitted with an arrestor wire held a couple of inches into the air by iron blocks. It was a very small patch of runway, barely a hundred yards long, and it now dawned on us just how very minute a carrier flight deck is, out in the middle of the ocean. From the air it looked like a patch of carpet, and even at low landing speeds an aircraft would pass over the whole length in a few seconds. Overlooking the airfield was a concrete control tower with a tiny observation cabin on top, reached by a vertical iron ladder. From this, one could watch the trainee pilots – our future chauffeurs – attempting to place their Swordfish neatly on that tiny patch of 'deck', praying that the hook at the rear of the aircraft would catch the wire, and that the pilot would cut the throttle at the right moment so that the aircraft would drop onto the ground in a three-point (all three wheels at once) attitude. Rather too often for our comfort, we'd see them rolling beyond the limits of the pale concrete, out onto the black 'sea'. It didn't help to learn that the pilots being trained for work with us in 'TSR' (torpedo spotter reconnaissance) squadrons were, by one measure, the second-best group – the star students having been selected as naval fighter pilots. (We would learn to put that thought out of mind soon enough, and to be exceedingly grateful for their skills.)

Arbroath airfield sits on a low rise in the Angus landscape immediately behind the town. The wind sweeps in off the North Sea, but sometimes the sea-mist or 'haa' would close over the airfield, obliterating everything. But when it cleared, across the rooftops and beyond the church spire, the sea glinted, waiting for us.

*

That sea almost claimed me early in my career. It was my first – for a long time, my only – experience of being attacked by another aircraft, and it was friendly fire.

Among the various aircraft we were introduced to was the Walrus, otherwise elegantly known as the 'Shagbat'. The Walrus was a small flying boat, one of the most ungainly objects to fly during the war, but strangely it was designed by R.J. Mitchell, creator of that truly elegant and efficient machine, the Spitfire. Like the Spitfire again, the Walrus was rather successful. Originally produced by Mitchell's employers, Supermarine, production was subcontracted to Saunders-Roe at Cowes, who built over four hundred of them; I must have seen Shagbats there when doing the financial audits just before the start of the war.

The Walrus was a biplane with a single pusher propeller – that's to say, mounted backwards under the upper wing. It had the same radial Pegasus engine as a Swordfish, and so rarely failed its crew in mid-ocean. It looked thoroughly suited to the ocean; the rear cockpit had a neat sliding hatch, like something on a sailing dinghy, and the hull had the lines of a rather overweight canoe, with a little rudder at the stern, under the tailplane where the tail wheel would be on a Swordfish.

An FAA pilot, Terence Horsley, published in 1944 a modest book called *Find, Fix and Strike*. I still have my copy; I see from a pencilled mark that I paid 2/6d for it. Horsley asserted that his purpose was 'to foster a closer bond between the public and the Fleet Air Arm. The taxpayer is part owner, and we would like to hear him talking more about "our naval aircraft," and with a greater sense of proprietorship. The aircraft are his, and they are fighting his war.'

As part of his appeal to the British taxpayer, Horsley launches a courageous attempt to charm the public into appreciating some very unlikely planes. The aircraft, he admits are nothing very glamorous to look at, although 'they have been shot down by critics more often than they have by the enemy'. But the Walrus inspires his advocacy; he describes it as 'splashing around like a dignified Swan'. It had wonderfully sedate handling qualities:

> Turns are made with slow dignity, as one might imagine a
> 60-seater bus on a smooth road. Pipe and tobacco come out,
> the transparent panel is slid over our heads, but the side

window is left open for fresh air… On a rough day the
Walrus behaves more like a cow than a bus – a very friendly
cow, however…[5]

Shagbats were employed in reconnaissance, ferrying admirals
between each other's flagships, anti-submarine patrols, air-sea
rescue, even occasional dive-bombing. The Walrus was often fitted
to battleships, perched on a catapult on one of the gun turrets; when
it landed in the sea, terrified observers like myself had to climb out
of the cabin onto the upper wing (doing our best to avoid slithering
backwards into the blades of the propeller), where we would attach
a sling from one of the ship's derricks, for lifting back onto the
catapult – all as described in my *Manual of Seamanship*.

That autumn day I had been taken up in a Walrus for some
convoy-watching: a small flotilla was making its way in poor
weather south down the coast from Dundee. We cruised peaceably
beside it for a while at 85 knots, then turned back towards the Tay
– and suddenly we were being shot at! A fighter pounced on us
from the airfield at Crail in Fife – a Polish squadron, as we could
see from the red-and-white flash on the fuselage. He dropped on
us from the clouds, fired one machine-gun burst, then turned away;
thankfully he did not return, perhaps having seen our own British
markings even as he loosed off at us. The Walrus did have a
silhouette faintly similar to one of the small German flying boats,
but this was a case of fire first, look later.[6]

We were hit: one bullet had struck the valve rocker-box on one of
the pistons of our engine. A Pegasus could sometimes survive that;
there are records of motors with two pistons shot away continuing
to turn. But ours now fired only intermittently. Very quickly we lost
height, my pilot (a Royal Navy lieutenant) shouting, 'Bloody Poles!
Bloody, bloody Poles!' as we dropped into a very uncomfortable
landing, hopping and bouncing from wave-top to wave-top along
the Tay. Crail is little more than an hour's drive from Arbroath. I
hate to think of the telephone calls that evening.

*

One felt better for comradeship. There were some two dozen of us
on the training, a very mixed gang. One of the oddities of FAA

manning was that they had a recruiting office in New Zealand; it was such a remarkably efficient and zealous office that by the end of the war something like a quarter of FAA aircrew were New Zealanders. So, at Arbroath, I quickly made friends with Murray Richardson, a half-Maori who would eventually be best man at my wedding.

Of the others, one rather less pleasant man had been a stockbroker, and he continued trying to make his fortune each day on the telephone. He seemed to think about little else, regarding those of us who were irredeemably penniless as weak-willed; this rankled when I thought of my mother's long hours of dressmaking, while this man believed he could do it with a few phone calls. There were two schoolmasters also, one of them a physics teacher who frequently had to correct the instructor teaching us about the new ASV radar that everyone was just learning to use.

There were also three regular Royal Navy officers who had followed the 'proper' route through the Navy college at Dartmouth; they were the subject of a good deal of insubordinate behaviour and niggling. Trainee officer aircrew were called 'goons' and we let them know that they were goons like the rest of us. In our eyes, they were just recently graduated college boys, giving themselves RN airs that they did nothing to merit. Even when we were flying together in the same daily peril and discomfort, some of the RN officers would try to keep their superior distance, and some would affect eccentricities: a swagger stick, for instance.

In their eyes, the rest of us were just matelots – naval airmen second class for the first two months, and after that, merely leading naval airmen, no better than leading seamen or engine room artificers or somesuch. But we all wore the same uniform of the naval officer cadet, with little to distinguish it from any rating's rig except that our neckerchief had a single white band instead of three narrow stripes, and our caps had a broad white capband. There was nothing to show that the 'regular men' were any different from the rest of us. It made them grind their teeth whenever 'that bloody man Le Page' came top of a test – as, in my perfectionist way, I tended to do. For all that, though, I envied their social ease; I was still the Eltham boy, the one who had bought the wrong hat for work at the accountants. I was making good here, I was getting on; I was determined not to let myself down. I made a point of smart appearance, and kept my south-east London voice on a tight rein in their vicinity. Envy became resentment, and so I avoided them; we did not socialize.

With my New Zealand friend Murray, however, I went 'ashore' whenever I could – 'ashore' being anywhere outside the 'ship' that was the Arbroath Naval Air Station. We began a habit of going to the Church of Scotland for Sunday matins, where we were befriended by one of the church wardens, who would invite us home for coffee or lunch. Ernie Myles was a man of importance in Arbroath, both in the kirk and the 'toon hoos' (town hall). He also had two lovely daughters my own age. I might not be good enough for the RN officers, but I could take tea with the church warden's daughters. Sometimes, flying above the town, I would gaze down from the Shark or Swordfish and fancy that I could see them in the garden below.

But it was a town of stern, firm morals, not to be trifled with. The minister of the kirk would flash his eyes from the pulpit and, week by week, deliver an almost identical sermon. He warned us of the coming invasion, and beseeched us to be on our guard and ready to fight to the last, for our very souls were in peril. He did not mean Hitler and the Germans: he meant the Papists. There were Romish hordes waiting to swarm across the Channel on the coat-tails of the Nazis, and if we did not resist they would surely enslave us in a false faith and drag us to our doom.

*

Sobered by these reflections, I went down to the Arbroath post office and addressed a telegram to Gina, my London girlfriend: 'Will you marry me?'

'That will be one shilling and fourpence,' said the postmistress. 'What if she says no? You'll have wasted your money.'

Letting the Commanding Officer of the Arbroath training school know that I wanted to get married in May 1942 immediately laid me open to several weeks of blackmail. Any extra duty that could be dumped on a trainee officer seemed to come my way. It was also made clear that, if I did not do exceedingly well in my exams, performing well above average, there were many ways in which the wedding could be postponed.

So, it would seem that I had the clearest possible incentive for performing brilliantly in those exams – were it not for one thing: I was already unpopular with the regular officers on the course, not just the regular Dartmouth boys in my group but a number of others more senior who saw me as getting above myself. I was in a bind: I studied furiously, while trying my best to be especially polite to everyone. Now, sixty years later, I still have a strong visual and emotional memory of walking along the corridor to the navigation exam, making a silent vow: 'I am not going to make a single mistake.' It was a re-run of my School Certificate chemistry practical at Christ's Hospital, and once again the strong desire to 'get on' took hold of me. I came out top of the course and was congratulated by the CO – to the disgust of the regular Navy officers.

And so I got married on Sunday 12 April 1942 (*plate 2*).

With Murray from New Zealand, I left Arbroath – putting Ernie the church elder's lovely daughters firmly behind me – and returned to London, to Eltham and to Holy Trinity church. My family were there, and two friends from the Arbroath course. A dozen old friends and neighbours came, and there was also a colleague from Barton Mayhew, Chartered Accountants. His name was Matthew, and he was enormously fat. This was the man with whom I had viewed flying boats at Cowes, and throughout my time with the accountants, including on our delightful trips around the dairies and the cream teas of the West Country, he had shown a restrained but obvious affection for me. Now in the ceremony he made himself conspicuous by occupying an aisle seat; as Gina and I walked down the aisle past him, he ostentatiously drew from his pocket an enormous black-edged handkerchief, wiping at the corners of his eyes as if to dry his tears. Murray and I and our two Navy colleagues were not fully commissioned yet and so were in our uniforms as leading naval airmen. At the altar, the ring was passed to the vicar on my upturned matelot's cap with its white officer-cadet's capband.

Afterwards, the guests moved to the church hall to drink our health in beer and sweet sherry. That was that; wartime weddings were simple: it wasn't done to be showy in the country's time of need, and it would have tempting fate.

Bride and groom – ignorant, totally without experience – spent the wedding night at the Waldorf Hotel in the Aldwych. Then we had a week at a pub by the sea in the West Country. We went to bed very early…

We had left our suitcases at the foot of the bed without unpacking them completely, but with the lids open. In Gina's case there was a box of chocolates, nestling in a heap of tissue paper. Stark naked, we had embarked on our caresses when we became aware of a furtive rustling among the tissue. We froze, clinging to each other, and listened. Could it be… a Nazi spy? Or mice? Or worse, yes, yes, oh the horror, it undoubtedly was – a rat! We lay in the dark and listened and whispered and worked out a plan, an impossibly foolish plan, all my foolish idea. I was to creep to the end of the bed, while Gina would locate (in the dark) the cord of the overhead light switch. When I was in position, I was to shout *Now*! At this, Gina was to turn on the light, and I would leap down from the end of the bed and slam the lid of her suitcase shut, and then stand on it to trap the rat.

All went initially to plan. Moving exceedingly slowly, Gina groped in the blackness over our bed for the light cord, while I worked my way to the foot of the bed, standing in the dark ready to leap, wobbling somewhat on the mattress. I shouted my *Now!!!* and, as the light went on, I leapt in the direction of the suitcase, striking a posture of magnificent naked rat-slaughtering bravado, like something from a neo-classical painting. A terrified Gina, equally nude, jumped out of the bed to find a weapon with which to slay the rodent – and at this moment the landlord threw open our bedroom door to check the blackout (as he was legally required to do). What stupendous foreplay!

When we went down to breakfast in the morning, the other guests as one turned their faces in our direction, and stared. The story had clearly lost nothing in the landlord's retelling.

*

THE LUCK OF THE DEVIL

We duly passed our exams, and were commissioned as Temporary Acting Sub-Lieutenants (A), Royal Naval Volunteer Reserve – about as cautious and qualified a title as one could hope to acquire. One or two on the course had been 'dipped' (failed), and one or two others were too young for an officer's elevated dignity and had to spend some time as midshipmen first.

Now we passed out in a blaze of glory, in our new gold-braided uniforms. For just two weeks, I was sent to the Royal Naval College at Greenwich – very conveniently, as my in-laws' house was just a couple of miles away so that I had two weeks lodging with my wife. We were given a 'knife and fork' course – an introduction to the etiquette of the Navy officer-gentleman, so that a boy from the beer-and-ladders of Eltham might know how not to make a fool of himself in the wardroom. In the first of these talks, I was solemnly informed that, 'the word *fuck* is no longer part of your vocabulary'. (This lesson did not long survive operational duty.)

We were also given a course of lectures, which were really just a means of keeping us off the streets. Some of these could be very interesting, such as those on naval history given by members of the instructor branch of the Navy. Others were farcical if entertaining. There was, for instance, an elderly Commander RN who had read a book about Freud; he talked at some length about the sexual significance of his housemaid breaking the spout of his teapot.

There was strange company at Greenwich, whom we would join for lunch. There were a number of senior officers – refugees, really – from the navies of Allied countries that had already capitulated to the Germans. There was a group of Free French admirals, whose navy would soon be sitting ignominiously at the bottom of Toulon harbour (North Africa) where it was scuttled to prevent the Germans taking it over.[7] There was also King Peter of Yugoslavia,[8] and even King Zog of Albania.[9] They were tragic figures. The BBC tried to put heart into them by broadcasting, each evening before the *Six o'Clock News*, the 'National Anthems of the Allies'. As the war progressed, and more and more countries were either overrun by the Axis or were recruited by Britain and the United States, so the list of Allies grew and the number of anthems to be played became longer and longer. Italy had conquered Ethiopia, so

Ethiopia became our ally also; their anthem was exceedingly glamorous.

The pathos of all this was such that I wrote my first wartime verse:

> As each mad, martial melody trumpets out
> I see the tragedies of nations pass;
> The Polish cavalry, in bitter rout,
> Makes a last stand among the sun-weary grass.
> Frightened French peasants jam the country roads
> As merciless the silver bombers dive.
> Sad, frantic farmers jettison their loads
> And try to save themselves, at least, alive.

Which is what we would all be doing, soon enough.

Notes

1. By then, officially the Fleet Air Arm had been disbanded and the service was named the Air Branch of the Royal Navy. But then as now it remained familiar as the Fleet Air Arm.

2. The FAA pilot Terence Horsley was soon to write: 'It is a strange thing that the job of the observer is less keenly sought by recruits than the job of pilot. For there is no doubt which is the more important… Give me an observer who is trained in the Fleet Air Arm manner, and I will fly anywhere. Take him away, and I am a man of straw.' *Find, Fix and Strike* (1944).

3. As Cecil Lewis noted in his book on First World War flying, *Sagittarius Rising* (1936), it was as easy to get lost in the air as it was when walking in a forest, and once lost, it was hard not to panic. In most respects, after all, a Swordfish was little more than an overgrown Sopwith Camel.

4. The dummy flight deck is still there (2011), marked out in the runway of what is now RM Condor (Royal Marines) at Arbroath. The deck is clearly visible in aerial views; I walked across it, and saw the remnants of the arrestor wire fittings. The control tower is still there also, little changed in 2011. It is now a listed building.

5. There is a puzzle about this passage. I have Robert's copies both of Horsley's book and of *Wings of the Morning*, a history of the FAA by Ian Cameron (1965), which quotes the above description of the Walrus, attributing it to Horsley. But search Horsley's little book as I might, I cannot find the passage, and certainly not in the brief section describing FAA aircraft.

6. See the discussion of this incident in the Introduction, p.8-9. The date is uncertain. It seems possible that the Polish squadron involved was 309 'Land of Czerwien', based for a few months at Crail. It was a fighter-reconnaissance squadron that had originally flown Lysander spotters, but which at Crail was equipped with American P-41 Mustangs also; this had perhaps got the men over-excited. But the dates do not fit.

7. The mass scuttling eventually took place on 27 November 1942.

8. King Peter had the most glamorous ancestry Europe could provide, being descended from the Hohenzollerns, the Saxe-Coburgs, an infanta of Portugal and a princess of Russia. He fled Yugoslavia after the Axis invasion of April 1971. He came to Britain, finished a degree at Cambridge and then joined the RAF. In Yugoslavia, his supporters the 'Chetniks' soon switched from resisting the invaders to attempting to wipe out Tito's communist partisans. In 1943, the Allies gave their support to the partisans, and Peter was an increasingly isolated figure. He was officially deposed in 1945, moving to the USA, taking to drink and dying of cirrhosis of the liver in 1970.

9. Zog was the son of an Ottoman pasha. When the Ottoman Empire collapsed, in 1925 Zog became the first President of Albania, then a constitutional monarch in 1928, increasingly dependent on Italy. In April 1939, Mussolini's Italians invaded, quickly taking control. Zog and his family fled to Britain, living first at the Ritz and then a country estate. After the war, they moved first to Egypt and then to France, where Zog died in 1993.

CHAPTER THREE

The Action of the Tiger

No. 816 was a Swordfish squadron, originally formed in October 1939 within a few weeks of the outbreak of war. They were given nine Swordfish on the ageing carrier HMS *Furious*, and began by escorting one of the first supply convoys from Canada. They had not had an easy war so far. *Furious* and 816 Squadron had taken part in the despairing defence of Norway in April 1940, and had launched the first airborne torpedo strike of the Second World War; they had attacked German destroyers in Trondheim harbour, only to see the torpedoes hit an unnoticed sand-bar and explode.

The Norwegian campaign had been a disaster for the FAA. The feeble British dive-bombers – Skuas – had managed quite miraculously to sink a German cruiser, the *Königsberg*, but thereafter nothing had gone right. Attempting to defend shipping from the *Luftwaffe*, the FAA discovered that British 'fighters' were considerably slower than German bombers. In desperate attacks on Trondheim harbour, on Petsamo in Finland and on Kirkenes, aircraft after aircraft had been lost either to defence batteries or simply through running out of fuel as they struggled back towards their carriers. Some crashed into the sea with dry tanks after circling overhead waiting for *Ark Royal* to turn into the wind. Another carrier, *Glorious*, was caught and sunk by the *Scharnhorst* because it hadn't occurred to anyone that the squadron might provide its own air cover at sea.

Between unhappy trips to Norway, 816 Squadron had received an urgent call to go and prop up another doomed campaign: the defence of France. The Swordfish were sent briefly to operate out of Jersey, doing what they could to defend the Dunkirk beaches, even operating against tanks. But Jersey became untenable. So 816 Squadron returned to HMS *Furious* and, in September that year, had a go at sinking *Scharnhorst*, but were driven off. A week or two later they were sent to make another suicidal daylight attack on

Trondheim harbour – and lost five aircraft and their crews. They did a little better in October, bombing fuel tanks at Tromsø.

In March 1941, 816 Squadron was seconded to RAF Coastal Command for mine-laying along the Dutch and French coasts. In June they were back on HMS *Furious* escorting convoys taking RAF to the besieged fortress of Malta. In November they were embarked on *Ark Royal*, returning from Malta – but before they reached Gibraltar, they were spotted by *U-81* and torpedoed. *Ark Royal* sank, and 816 Squadron temporarily ceased to exist.

*

In February 1942, 816 Squadron re-formed at Palisadoes, Jamaica (a curious coincidence: much of my academic career post-war centred on Jamaica). Shortly afterwards they came to Britain on yet another carrier (HMS *Avenger*) and fetched up at Lee-on-Solent at HMS Daedalus. And there I joined them, at long last qualified as an officer and air observer, in exactly the place where I had first put on a matelot's sea-going rig more than a year previously.

There was another odd coincidence: the senior observer of the squadron (usually known as 'Sobs') was called Charles Simpson. He had been one of the first recruits at the new Metropolitan Police College set up at Hendon in the 1930s, after which he'd been the bobby on the beat in Crown Woods Way, Eltham – Gina's road. It had been his custom when he came off duty to go to the house of two pretty girls at the top of the street, hang his helmet in the hall and settle down to a gin-and-tonic and a game of Monopoly. (After the war, we heard that Charles became vicar of a secluded parish in the west of Ireland).

The Commanding Officer of 816 Squadron was a Captain of Marines, Olly Patch DSO, DSC, who had distinguished himself in the attack on Taranto harbour by sinking with a single torpedo[1] two Italian submarines and the tanker they were refuelling from – an unequalled hat-trick. It was typical of the makeshift nature of the FAA that our CO was a flying enthusiast who had talked his way across from the Marines. We had several more New Zealanders also.

But when would we be assigned to an aircraft carrier? Not yet:

we were nominated for work in the Channel – which meant that we were promptly sent back to Scotland for more training, to Macrihanish by Campbeltown on the Mull of Kintyre, a very long way from anywhere. There we were to learn how to navigate at night, something that seemed to have been missed out in the previous year of training. We trained, we practised and we waited. No. 816 was one of the first squadrons to be equipped with anti-submarine rockets (instead of depth charges), eight of these on racks under the lower wing: so we spent many hours attacking smoke floats with rockets. As a variation, we attacked the wildlife with smoke floats; from the air, we could see scores of basking sharks cruising slowly about the sea lochs, just below the surface, and we would try to dive-bomb them. The sharks took no notice whatever.

It was a ghastly posting. I took to verse again, addressing myself to the Sea Lords of the Admiralty:

Misery on the Mull

Dear Sirs,
If you will give me space,
I will inform the human race
About affairs so grave that I'm
compelled to put them into rhyme.
   At midnight, when the moon's pale light
Transforms this treeless, dreary site
Into a realm of strange delight,
I rise, and clothe myself for flight.
For hours and hours, it seems to me,
Over the cold, inviting sea
We wing our blithe and carefree way
Returning with the break of day.
Gladly I sip the unsweetened cup
Of cocoa, and more gladly sup
Off the carcases of murdered sheep.
I then resign myself to sleep.
   Four hours later, much refreshed
I rise again and, quietly dressed
In dressing gown of aftermath

I sally forth to take a bath.
But no! The aqueous autocrat
Who makes decisions about that
Has kept a heartening surprise
For those who dare late to arise
And, with his Wren (a plumber's daughter)
Has cut off all the bloody water.
    Never mind, chaps! Our hearts we steel
Thinking to find a toothsome meal
And winsome wenches bearing dishes
Cooked to gratify our wishes.
Patiently as we are able,
Seated at the breakfast table
We wait for twenty minutes more
While stewards quietly ignore
Our mute, appealing, hungry looks
And in the galley there, the cooks
Sip noisily at cups of tea
And fling their priceless repartee
At all who get their lugs to leeward
While trying to engage a steward.
    At last, with slow and ponderous gait,
A man approaches with a plate,
A dish heaped high with glutiny
At which a dog would mutiny –
A dish of brose. I ask for syrup –
The spectre gives a mirthless chirrup:
'Syrup's orf, Sir. Milk's all gorn.
Sugar ain't arrived this morn.
There was some marmalade at eight,
But that's gorn now, Sir. You're too late
For bacon and some nice fried bread,
But there's some 'addick now, instead.'
    Kind Sirs, in cold and seething rage,
I sign myself – R.B. Le Page.

This grim existence was a little relieved by the delights of flying –
and for some of us, by the curiosities of Kintyre social life. I had

found lodgings in a Macrihanish cottage with a Mrs McQueen and her batty teenage daughter, and I wrote to Gina begging her to join me.

I was a newly married man; I wanted to see my wife. On two occasions, Gina travelled up from London – which meant not only the long train journey to Glasgow but also the interminable drive along the narrow winding road down the Mull of Kintyre. She once did this in the Navy's laundry truck, stopping off everywhere to deliver pristine uniforms. On another occasion she flew: a little civil airline ran the service. It was the first time she'd ever flown anywhere.

One evening when Gina was there, I invited my squadron pals back for the evening; they arrived, bringing beer. Shortly afterwards, Gina went through to the kitchen to make coffee – and was accosted by Mrs McQueen:

'Mrs Le Page, would that be beer the young gentlemen are drinking?'

'I suppose it would be, Mrs McQueen.'

'Mrs Le Page, you will call your husband through, if you please. There has been no strong drink taken in this house in seventy years, and they'll not be taking it now. Your tenancy is terminated.'

She took a great deal of mollifying.

But in spite of the complete isolation of Macrihanish, the lack of anything resembling a glittering town centre, there were dinners to be had.

Or, at least, so my pilot Bobby discovered. Bobby Creighton was a Glaswegian – and of typically Glaswegian short stature – with a broad accent that I sometimes found quite difficult to understand. He got himself invited to a smart evening in Campbeltown. The only drawback was that we were also required to be flying that day, and the timing for his dinner was rather tight. Bobby therefore decided that, in order to save time, he would fly in his very smartest dress uniform under his Sidcot flying suit and, as soon as we landed, would jump out of the Swordfish and scuttle away in a borrowed car to dinner. That was all fine by me, and we took off with George our air gunner in the back seat, sailing away over some corner of the western isles.

All went fine until in mid-air Bobby decided that he needed a pee.

FAA flying suits were not designed for peeing. There was in some aircraft a pee-tube in the cockpit, but it often didn't work or it slipped or otherwise betrayed us, and anyway it was almost impossible to find one's way out of the uniform through all the layers of insulation. One way or another one came home wet.

'To hell with that,' said Bobby down the other rubber tube that joined us at the ears, 'I'm going out to dinner. I'm not wetting this uniform.'

'What are you going to do?' I piped back.

'I'm going to land,' he said.

'Where?' I cried in dismay.

'Down there.'

He pointed to the Isle of Arran. There was a beach below us, a pretty little beach, longer than the dummy landing strip at Arbroath. Before I could raise any objections, Bobby swung the Swordfish in a turn and down onto the bumpy, tide-ridged sand. As we trundled to a stop, he began to climb out of the cockpit – only to see that we now had company: a crofter and his teenage daughter.

They walked a little towards us, and stared in silence. 'Afternoon,' called Bobby, wondering how to explain his arrival on their island, and now desperate for his pee. 'Couple of quick repairs needed…' And he began fiddling with something nondescript on the underside of the Swordfish. Seeing this, the farmer and daughter overcame their reserve and came forward to offer assistance.

'No, no, err… thank you, no, well… excuse me a tick…'

He scampered into some nearby scrub. No one – neither me nor George our gunner nor the islanders – said a word; the taciturn crofters stood quite still, gazing at me. A moment later Bobby trotted back, grinning happily.

'Actually, if you wouldn't mind just helping us turn her about?' The beach was narrower and softer than he'd thought from the air. Between the five of us – aircrew and crofters – we'd be able to lift the canvas tail of the Swordfish and swing it right round.

'You'll bide a moment,' said the crofter, and disappeared back into his house at the shore's edge, re-emerging a moment later with a bottle of whisky.

'You're crazy,' I muttered to Bobby. 'What if we'd damaged the undercarriage?'

'Bullshit,' he retorted, 'and anyway, when did you last get invited out to dinner?'

*

Then, at the end of August 1942, all of a sudden and after more than a year of training, we were at war.

We had still imagined that any day now we would be assigned to an aircraft carrier, to make a reality of all those simulated deck landings on the Arbroath concrete. But there were no escort carriers available – they were being built as fast as possible in the USA, but had not turned up yet – and so the posting that came through was to the South Coast, to RAF Thorney Island. We were not even under naval control, but subsumed into RAF Coastal Command, to spend our time laying mines in the Channel.

There was a bitterness in the very idea of Swordfish in the Channel. In February that year, a squadron of Swordfish unsupported by any fighter cover had attempted to stop the battle-cruisers *Scharnhorst* and *Gneisenau* from making their celebrated 'Channel Dash' from the French port of Brest up to Kiel, from where they could both menace North Atlantic convoys and also defend Norway. That squadron – 825 – had been wiped out in the attempt. So now we were somehow to make up for the blunder by scattering mines in front of the French and Dutch ports, in particular Le Havre and Cherbourg.

We knew about the Channel Dash; everyone did. We knew that, while there was no end to the perils in flying off tiny escort carriers in the North Atlantic – torpedoes, storms, running out of fuel too far from the ship – there was one danger we would not face out in mid-ocean: there would be no German fighter aircraft and scarcely any anti-aircraft fire. Over the Channel, the greatest weakness of the Swordfish was exposed: faced or chased by a modern fighter, we stood no better chance of survival than had the doomed aircrews of 825 Squadron.

The squadron that went to Thorney Island consisted of eight crews (that is, eight each of pilots, observers and air gunners) and six aircraft. We had with us also our own troops: nearly eighty of them, the specialist riggers and fitters on whom we relied.

I have a photograph taken of us at Thorney Island in October 1942, a few weeks after we'd arrived (*plate 3*). There in the front row is cheerful and heroic Olly Patch in his rather obviously different uniform of Marines, with his red setter on a lead and a crudely painted piece of cardboard daubed *816 Sqdn* with the date. Next to him sits Charles Simpson, still looking like a policeman, unsmiling and neatly turned out. My good friend Don Ridgway beams and slouches. Bobby and George Loosemore our TAG (telegraphist air gunner) are there near me, George looking young, tall and handsome, with his cap swept well back in a manner rather frowned upon. I stand at the extreme left, slightly detached. I look belligerent, my feet slightly apart, my arms clasped tightly across my chest, somewhat arrogant and defiant in my new-found officer status, nothing like a humble junior clerk from Eltham, for now I had 'got on'. But the stance does nothing for my uniform.

We had trained and trained and trained – but of all of us, only the Commanding Officer and the two RN observers had any operational experience. Although at Macrihanish we had done as much night-flying as possible, still for most of us this amounted to no more than perhaps a dozen hours.

To begin with I was the only married officer, although Olly Patch got married not long after our arrival. I had to get Olly's permission to live ashore (that is, not on the aerodrome) and to find somewhere for me and Gina to stay in connubial joy when I wasn't flying. I stood in front of Olly thoroughly agitated as he read through the regulations – until he told me sharply to relax, while he found a loophole.

I did the rounds of estate agents in Emsworth, the small town near the aerodrome, and found a small three-bedroomed semi on a lane leading from the base in the direction of Chichester. I could just afford the rent on my sub-lieutenant's pay, when I added my extra flying allowance. A week later, Gina gave up her job in

Martin's Bank in London and joined me. We settled down to wedded bliss.

What an illusion. Only now, writing this fifty-eight years later, do I realize quite how much I underestimated the stress she was living under, having herself only a vague idea what was happening to her new husband, flying night after night.

But I did start to put into verse something of our lives at the time, in a poem called *A Night's Work*:

Beyond the drawing room windows, the dusk
Deepened over the tiny garden.
The shades of a November evening
Came stalking inland across the marshes.
Bonfire smoke curled upward and died.
A sudden gust stirred dead leaves,
Then it, too, died, gave way to quiet.
The drab trees shrugged, and were still.
Down by the creek, the silent tide
Drove the seabirds before it over the mudflats,
Lapped at drying dinghy hulls,
Lifted them buoyantly on its back
And passed on as they danced in the dusk
Daemonic with the water beneath them.
Beyond the harbour, heaving rollers
Flung purple spray to the horizon.
Over Pompey town, portly steel-grey
Barrage balloons bluffed the twilight.

Robert sighed, stretched, rose from his seat
By the drawing room fire. His wife, fawn-like
Twined her long arms nervously round him,
Nuzzled her face in his neck
While the fear that had become her familiar
Leered at her from the corner behind him.
It would pluck her sleeve for the rest of the evening,
Pace the lonely bedroom later,
Hold back the hands of the kitchen clock,
Spin out the slow hours of the night

    Until the click of the garden gate
    And Robert's step in the early morning
    Would banish it, her heart leaping
    With joy at her lover's safe return…

Those mine-laying operations – our first warlike duty – were a strange mixture of the tediously routine and endlessly tense and dangerous.

As I cycled from our cottage back to the squadron in the failing autumn light, I would pass through the tangle of briar, bramble and hawthorn that surrounded the airfield, in amongst which the Swordfish – now painted a strange and creepy matt black for night flying – would be standing concealed, already armed with their load of sea mines. These were fitted with magnetic delayed-action triggers; they were set only to go off when a dozen or more ships had passed over them, so that (in theory) minesweepers would have 'cleared' the area, after which grander victims would supposedly sail to their doom. The mines weighed nearly a ton; a Swordfish with one of those slung beneath her was less than sprightly. They gave the aircraft's silhouette a sinister heaviness in the dusk, like a devilish hen brooding on eggs. Another flight might be about to leave, and I would glimpse the mechanics perched on the undercarriage struts, cranking furiously at the starter handles; every few moments as I passed there would be a cry of 'Contact!' heralding a cough and splutter from the Pegasus, a shaft of flame spitting backwards from the exhaust, and the roar of the engine at full throttle, the backdraft from the propeller lashing the grass flat and bludgeoning the hawthorn and bramble bushes and myself, passing on my cycle.

In the operations room we'd receive our detailed instructions – very detailed, because mines had to be laid very precisely in the French harbours, positioned in the dredged channels followed by the shipping; anywhere else, they were wasted. Next, a jovial, well-meaning and rather myopic gentleman from RAF Intelligence would blink at us as we entered, tucking our caps under our arms. He wasn't so well used to naval squadrons; the RAF aircrews saluted and were rather more receptive to the information he offered. Already, we FAA crews seemed to think that we knew more than he did of the moles and the gun emplacements of the port defences, of the safest ways in and out of the target. We had been operational only weeks, but had firm notions already about how to go 'gardening'. The intelligence man would have his say, tell us the latest and hold his peace, wishing us luck and mentioning carrier pigeons for messages in case we were shot down, but we'd laugh at the old joke (already, it seemed an old joke) and reply, 'No room!'

Then we'd saunter next door to flirt with the WAAF girls who gave us our escape gear and survival rations. We'd leave the ghostly fluorescent lighting of the rations issue room and move into the single naked bulb of the crew room, climb into our Sidcot suits, our Mae West life jackets and flying boots, stuffing the boots and every available pocket with chocolate, torches and slide-rules, before waddling out to the waiting transport trucks to be trundled round the perimeter road to our own aircraft, and our turn with the mechanics and the crank handles.

Now we would feel the tension as we eased into the tiny cramped cockpits, clipping ourselves to our parachutes, checking the compass, the lights, the airspeed indicator and the cathode ray tube of the ASV radar. The fitters all swore that the radar would sterilize me, sitting for hours with ten thousand volts between my knees. Behind me, the air gunner would be uncovering his Vickers, checking the gas-operated mechanism of the machine gun, loading it, stashing spare drums of ammunition below his seat, then tinkering with the radio, his other job. We would stash the other essentials also: coffee, sandwiches, tucked away for the homeward trip. Settled, we'd fasten goggles, helmet, plug in our radio microphones and our rubber speaking-tubes, waiting for the light from the control tower telling us to begin taxiing, while all three of us listened intently to the note of the Pegasus engine on which we depended. And at last we'd turn onto the runway – few lights anywhere now – and surge away into the blackness; as the winter hardened, we would be bumping over frozen mud, which could sometimes snap off the aircraft's tail wheel. But on the runway, the tail would lift almost immediately, and only yards later the pilot would haul back on the stick and we'd see the small blue lights of the airfield perimeter flash beneath us.

Nose up now, climbing for the cloud base, we would circle and I would set course from the airfield beacon, estimate wind speed and direction from the appearance of the white horses on the water, just discernible as we crossed the coast. Then I'd take a bearing from the usually visible Selsey Bill. At night and near to the enemy, there was no possibility of using our smoke-float procedure to calculate our speed over the sea; I would have to pray that the Met reports were accurate as to the windspeed and direction. Navigating by feeble torchlight, I would push the goggles off my face to peer at the chartboard on my knees, and at once my naked eyes would begin to weep and stream.

'Course two-one-four, Bobby!'

'Two-one-four, OK, on course.'

I'd check the time, take bearings and plot the landfall, and then at last pull my goggles back over my eyes and, for a while, relax and think.

Sometimes, flying through the night, having set course and sitting in silence behind the roar of the Pegasus, I would glimpse another aircraft in the distance and would wonder where they were going. I would think that we should go close to them, hail them and ask them for the news.

After a while, I would become alert again and start glancing at my watch by the light of the radar's cathode ray tube.

'Stand by to turn, Bobby, two-nine-0, then down to 100 feet. OK… turn.'

As the port wings lifted steeply I'd stare straight down into the void to starboard through the purple glow of the exhaust as we swung into a shallow dive at 100 knots. Now we were dependent on Bobby's flying skill; our barometric altimeters were not reliable at 100 feet, and in the dark the pilots found that they could be near-hypnotized by peering at the glossy blackness below.

The ASV (air-to-surface vessel) radar saved us often: it could pick out coastline as a ragged edge, and also any shipping in front of us. The ASV sent a signal straight ahead of the Swordfish, which then bounced back off anything solid and returned to be collected by antennas on the wings to port and starboard. This was displayed on the cathode ray tube between my knees as blips of varying size to left or right of a central line. If the object was to starboard, the blip would be larger on the right side of centre, and as we turned towards it, the blips would become equal. On the radar I might see both the jagged etching of the shore, and in front of it a tiny blip – a French trawler perhaps? Defying the fact of war...

'Dead ahead four miles, Bobby, something small down on the sea.'

We were almost at sea-level ourselves.

George the gunner would now be swinging his Vickers over the side but I would motion him not to fire: no point in calling attention to ourselves... until lazy red-yellow tracer curved up ahead of us and everything crashed onto the decking as Bobby made a tight turn to starboard, pushing the throttle wide open and easing the stick back to avoid smashing into the sea.

'OK, chum, back on course,' I'd instruct him. 'You've upset the coffee.'

'Fuck the coffee,' he'd retort, forgetting that the word was no longer part of our vocabulary.

He'd throttle back, saying: 'Broken water ahead. There's Cherbourg mole. Hold your tits now.'

We would drop to fifty feet, the maximum mine-laying height. I would sense Bobby fiddling with the switches, arming the mine and the release mechanism. Now we'd be tense again, skidding over the wave-tops into Cherbourg's main shipping channel, wishing the engine was quieter. Pencils of light would leap vertically right in front of us, sweeping left and right – another, and another – creating a lattice around us. Always, my reflexes would force me to duck, and I would sometimes laugh coldly at the thought that my white face must shine like a moon in the searchlight beam – so I would hide it behind the canvas side of the Swordfish. Now shells would start bursting, rather beautiful hand-sized puffs, with the beads of tracer weaving about us like an obscene ballet.

Rocked by the bursts we'd fly on through this light show, saved in the main by flying too low and too slow for the anti-aircraft guns' predictors. As the mine dropped, the plane – freed of that deadweight – would leap forward, while Bobby pushed the throttle wide open, turning in a steep bank over the heads of the Germans, while George behind me turned the Vickers on them. Then into our agreed getaway course and down towards the water again, much safer there.

I could now check my watch by the reflection of the searchlights on the underside of the blanket of cloud. When well clear of the harbour, we would at last climb for cloud-cover. On and on over the fleecy blue-white moonlit strato-cumulus.

I would be near numb with cold now, but often felt remarkably tranquil, my fear and tension soothed by the starlight, often thinking of the jostling and lying, the cheating and aggression of the world below us, all distant for a while.

God, it was cold, though. I'd stamp my feet on the boards. Behind me, George would pour more coffee. Now we would feel tired and mortal, needing soft blankets and sleep. There was something in Shakespeare: 'To be imprisoned in the viewless winds…'

As we approached the friendly coast, we'd begin to fantasize about bacon and eggs sizzling in the warm mess.

'Five miles, Bobby. Down to one thousand.'

No answer, but the stick going forward, the nose down, the cloud coming up to meet us. Then down through the swirling grey-black vapours – always a scary moment, this. Though there were no mountains here, still there were the sea cliffs, and the downs inland, and we had all heard of too many aircraft flying in cloud slap into a hillside. I'd hope that the Met reports were accurate: *Cloud-base two thousand*. Also that the information I had on the Portsmouth barrage balloons (a mere four miles from Thorney Island) was up-to-date.

At last, Bobby would turn on his lights, port and starboard, little patches of coloured fire in the frost. Clouds now above us, breakers beneath, white flecks in ink. Behind me, George would ship his gun and give a raised thumb. I'd be able to see my toy house at the edge of the aerodrome, see the frozen chrysanthemums in the front garden, the windows and even the tattered curtains of the tiny kitchen, and would imagine my wife waiting and listening for us.

And there in the mess would be the other aircrew, still in fleece-lined boots and battledress, stretched out around a blazing fire with pipes and pints of beer, puffing and dozily talking over the night.

Finally, with the cloud clearing, I'd cycle home by moonlight. A drowsy challenge at the guardhouse, and a reassurance.

'Goodnight, sir. Glad you're safe back.'

And sometimes, as I pedalled home, looking through the moon's gleam across the frosted sedge grasses by the creek, I'd stop and see swans – fifty, or almost a hundred, white on the dark water – feeding silently on the mere as the mist lifted in soft layers over the marshes.

*

But not everyone did come back. To our horror, we lost more and more aircraft and crew. On our very first mine-laying operation, against the heavily defended harbour at Cherbourg, two Swordfish went down. One was piloted by our one RN officer, 'Dook' Norfolk, who wore on his uniform a DSC that he'd won in Swordfish operations against the Italians in the Western Desert.

Our tactics had been wrong. We had agreed to go in one at a time at an interval of ten minutes. This was a mistake, a bit of tidiness that the Germans entirely appreciated. Thereafter, we flew separately and at irregular timings throughout the night; if nothing else, this would keep the gun crews round the harbour sleepless and on edge, the recurrent air-raid sirens leaving them exhausted and angry.

Which was how we were beginning to feel. One of the aircrew lost was that young, cheerful and very blond midshipman called Murray Pennington, whose fiancée Joan had stayed with us at our little house by the base. Another of our Swordfish came home too low over the cliffs one night, and flew into the Portsdown Hills behind the aerodrome. The observer in that one was a particular friend of mine, a very tall New Zealander called Jock Douglas. He was so tall that it proved difficult to find a coffin long enough.

I had by now something of a name as the squadron intellectual – or at least, I became the squadron letter-writer. It fell to me to write a description of Jock's funeral to send to his parents in New Zealand. (We kept up the correspondence for several months, and they came to see me after the war.) So one carried one's own fear, and other people's too. Yet another casualty was an Australian, Spud Tate, also known by his common oath: Jeez...

It was too much. We had been elaborately and lengthily trained to fly convoy escorts off carriers, and now the squadron was being destroyed before we could even begin. Cycling back to the aerodrome one afternoon in October 1942, I was passed by a squadron car going rather fast in the opposite direction. At the wheel was Olly Patch, the CO, with, sitting beside him, Charles Simpson, our senior observer. They were on their way to Portsmouth to make their views know to the Commander-in-Chief.

For his trouble, Patch was relieved of his command. That photo of the squadron, with Olly Patch and his dog, was taken the day he stood down.

*

The replacement CO was Lieutenant Ralph Stallard-Penoyre, RN. Apart from him and Charles Simpson, we were now an entirely RNVR squadron.

We now took on another job, in addition to mine-laying. The Germans had a number of armed merchantmen that they were using as raiders and that they were trying to move from the Baltic to Brest and other French ports by sailing down the Channel in a series of fast hops on dark, moonless nights. The penultimate hop would be from Le Havre to Cherbourg, which was 816 Squadron territory. We were sometimes alerted to these forays by messages from the French resistance; when this happened we were instructed to patrol all night in three-hour relays, find the raiders, bomb or torpedo them if we could, and alert the Navy's destroyers.

My friend Don Ridgway was the observer on the first of these missions. At around 9 p.m. his Swordfish (armed with 250lb bombs) was flying some five miles off the French coast and fifteen miles out of Le Havre, heading for Cherbourg, when Don glimpsed on his radar screen the faint outlines of the armed merchantman and five escorting E-boats (motor torpedo boats). They flew up-wind of the group of ships and dropped a parachute flare, and were delighted to see the flotilla suddenly, starkly illuminated. The discipline of the Germans was impeccable; although now brightly lit, their gunners held their fire – and the moment the flare went out, they were invisible in the darkness.

But they had been spotted by the Swordfish, and had been reported. Although the flight of aircraft standing by with torpedoes were grounded by deteriorating weather, a flotilla of Royal Navy destroyers intercepted the enemy, sinking the armed raider and four of the five E-boats.

There was now, at last, some sense of being useful.

Two days later, Don had a rather different experience. Again, he and his pilot were patrolling, searching the night with their radar. Again, Don saw the outlines on his screen. He once again directed Pete the pilot to fly up-wind, and again shouted at him to drop a flare – and at this moment (he and Pete confessed afterwards) thoughts of commendations and medals crept into their heads. They were rapidly disabused of that happy notion: within seconds, there was tracer and heavy anti-aircraft fire rising up at them from all directions, and three powerful searchlights had caught the Swordfish. Flying at just 1,500 feet, they were near-blinded by the lights but could just make out through the glare that the 'convoy' spotted by Don was, in fact, a muddle of various jetties jutting out at Le Havre, with boats of all sorts at anchor in the River Seine. They had provoked a full-scale air-raid defence.

Pete the pilot was a tennis player; he had powerful wrists. He hauled back on the stick and the Swordfish began to climb as steeply as was possible without stalling, clawing up towards the cloud. The searchlights clung on, but as usual the gun crews below could not credit the low speed of the Swordfish, or that an aircraft could turn so neatly, and their fire passed ahead of the plane. For the aircrew, it was the most terrifying three minutes of their careers. As they clambered into the clouds and turned away, they could see behind them the colourful tracer still stabbing upwards.[2] Now Pete flew at full throttle to get clear but in all the dodging and evading had so disconcerted his gyro-compass that, when Don looked at his own magnetic compass, he realized that they were flying north-east – into France! For the remainder of the patrol, he kept them on course for home by shouting directions down the rubber voice-tube.

Each operation provided its own scares, alarms and interest. The downside of the airworthiness of the Swordfish was that we were expected to fly in almost any weather – but to return safely, we must at least be able to see our home. If we couldn't find somewhere to land, there was only one alternative: to climb to several thousand feet, and bale out with parachutes. Throughout the autumn months, fogs and sea mists swirled over the coast, blinding us or requiring a re-routing. An RAF Meteorology officer came to brief us for an operation; he was more used to speaking to the crews of long-range bomber patrols. He announced that there was a risk of the weather deteriorating and he suggested that in this case we should divert to Stornoway in the Hebrides. We stared at him for a moment, then shouted in mockery that, given a following wind, a Swordfish could perhaps make Stornoway in eight hours, always provided that we could land and refuel halfway.

In the depths of that winter, one flight crew (Don Ridgway was again the observer) was redirected from Thorney Island to RAF Tangmere. At Tangmere, they had been fitted out with the newest thing in fog-dispersal equipment, called FIDO: petrol flaring from pipes alongside the tarmac. Tangmere had particular drawbacks for us. The RAF always did get the newest equipment, while the FAA creaked along in some earlier epoch. We had, as yet, no true radio-telephone equipment in the Swordfish, only Morse – but RAF Tangmere had given up on Morse as obsolete. Thorney Island rang them up on the phone to tell them that Swordfish were coming. Tangmere did not think to mention, however, that their field was being used that night by RAF Bomber Command. They had begun sending Lancasters to bomb northern Italy; this being rather beyond their maximum range (even with smaller bomb loads and long-range fuel tanks), the Lancasters could barely make it home to the south coast. As Don's Swordfish arrived, there were several Lancasters circling overhead. When all the Lancasters seemed to be down, they received what they thought was an approving lamp signal from below, and they brought the Swordfish in – only to be followed an instant later by a damaged Lancaster. The huge bomber was in total darkness; over Lombardy, with its gunners hard at work, the Lancaster had been hit by a single shell that had severed something electrical. With the jolt of meeting the ground, its lights suddenly flared and its turret guns began blazing again, as it bore down on the little Swordfish on the runway just ahead.

I remember another power cut. We shared with two other squadrons (811 and 819) the work of maintaining these night patrols – which meant that some nights we were off duty and free to be frivolous. On one such night Gina and I had invited all the aircrew for an impromptu party, a snack supper and a beer. Gina had managed to create some little cheese pies out of our meagre rations, and beer was plentiful enough, so we were mellowing nicely when the power failed. These cuts were not infrequent; the cables were slung across the road on wobbly poles and it only took a few cows deciding to scratch themselves to interrupt the supply. Undeterred, we continued by candlelight. But there came a squeal of brakes and a scrunching of wheels outside, and the Duty Officer's voice bellowing:

'Come on, boys – they're out!'

An RAF Hudson on patrol had spotted two German warships leaving Le Havre and heading for Cherbourg. Stallard-Penoyre, knowing that virtually the entire squadron was at my house, had agreed to set up a torpedo attack. As we bundled unsteadily out of the house, Gina was left at the door in the darkness wondering if she would ever see any of us again.

We had never done a torpedo attack. We had rehearsed such things *ad nauseam* at Arbroath and Macrihanish, flying low over the sea in formation, but we had no idea whether we could do it for real. In the operations room we heard that further reports were expected. We waited. We drank coffee, trying to sober up, while we studied charts and silhouettes of the enemy. The CO and the pilots worked out how we would approach, who would drop the flares and where, and how the attack would follow. The time crawled past; we began to feel very weary. Finally, in the early hours of the morning the RAF Hudson crew confessed that what they had thought were warships were probably just two large trawlers. We were stood down, and in a mixture of relief and rage we lay down to sleep there in the base.

It seemed to me that my head had just touched the pillow when a steward was shaking me:

'Sir! Sir! Your wife wants you on the phone.'

Cursing the day, I staggered along the corridor behind him in my underwear, and picked up the telephone. A tearful voice at the other end:

'Oh darling – thank God! – Are you all right, then?'

My answer was unforgivable:

'Of course I'm all right! What did you want to wake me up for?'

She had been awake all night until finally plucking up her courage to walk down the lane to the public telephone box. All too slowly I understood that I was not the only one under strain.

The episode had one other consequence. No. 816 Squadron had a coat of arms with a picture of a beast of prey and the heroic (Shakespearean) legend: *Imitate the Action of the Tiger*. Now the ground crews quietly repainted this to read: *Pissed but Willing*. We took it on as our motto. It was the sort of bravado young men needed.

There were plenty of other mishaps. One very dark night, a Swordfish mistook Langstone harbour for Thorney Island, and landed carefully in the water. Another took off for mine-laying at Cherbourg but for some reason could not get rid of the mine: it was stuck. So they had to bring it back, fully armed, and were diverted to Ford airfield. There, a technician climbed into the cockpit, decided that the problem was a blown fuse, and inserted a new one at which, with a loud clang, the mine fell off beneath the parked aircraft ... but didn't go off.

I wrote another poem; it carried an echo of my earlier solemn rhyme concerning the French peasants trying to stay alive in the *Blitzkrieg*:

Twenty Years On

What did you do in the war, Daddy?
What did you do in the war?
(*Don't disturb your father, dear –*
We've heard it all before...)
   I was a pilot, sonny,

One of the dauntless few.
You may think that sounds funny,
But listen while I tell you…

Did you fly a Spitfire, Daddy,
A snorting, fiery steed
With eleven hundred horsepower
And (for those days) quite a speed?
    No, I flew a Stringbag, sonny.
    We cruised at eighty-two.
    You may think that sounds funny,
    But listen while I tell you…

Was that a bomber, Daddy,
With a crew of seven inside
And a long, deep cavernous bomb-bay
With bomb-doors gaping wide?
    Yes, it was a bomber, sonny,
    But the only thing that gaped
    Was the cockpit top, where the wind shrieked
    And moaned like a woman raped.
    We carried six two-fifties
    Strung from the lower plane,
    And we never knew, when we took off,
    How we would land again.

What of the others, Daddy?
You've not told of those
Brave gunners in their turrets,
Bomb-aimer in the nose.
    Now, just keep quiet, sonny,
    And pull your finger out.
    Remember, it's a Stringbag
    That I'm telling you about.
    We carried an Observer, a gallant fellow he,
    Who drew lines on a chartboard
    Which he balanced on his knee.
    He'd wireless sets all round him,
    And wireless sets beneath.

To navigate he had to hold
A torch between his teeth.
The Gunner had a single gun
He did not dare to use.
It scarcely would have harmed the Hun
And merely caused abuse.
Those were the tough days, sonny,
When nightly, without fail,
We'd lay a mine in Cherbourg
And live to tell the tale.

Some two years later, I completed a long poem about these missions, a fragment of it quoted above ('A Night's Work', p.61). It was addressed to two of my colleagues. But I didn't show it to them, nor told them of my feelings. One didn't – not then.

Notes

1. Some accounts such as Ian Cameron's *Wings of the Morning* (1965) say that Captain Patch was carrying bombs.
2. The FAA pilot Terence Horsley, in his 1944 book *Find, Fix and Strike*, recalls this flak vividly: 'Much of it was obviously old French stock. Who but the Gauls would use orange, green, violet and gentian tracer?'

CHAPTER FOUR
Dasher

In early 1943, they found us an aircraft carrier. At Thorney Island, all we knew about her was that she was called HMS *Dasher*, and that she was small.

The Battle of the Atlantic – a battle fought to protect the supply convoys bringing food and armaments to Britain – had reached a peak in 1942; in November of that year alone, 128 ships had been torpedoed and sunk by U-boats. The Allied answer was air cover, and to carry the aircraft a bizarre collection of vessels – the escort carriers – appeared in American shipyards: some were oil tankers with a flight deck poised on top; some were the unfinished hulls of future merchant vessels hastily commandeered and topped-out as carriers; some were purpose-built but primitive steel tubs fabricated in sections often far from the sea, then assembled at a shipyard, spot-welded end to end. Some were simple conversions of merchantmen, known as banana-boats because the first of these had been contrived from a captured German ship (the *Hanover*), which had indeed carried fruit to Hamburg.[1] These escort carriers were designated CVE, which came to be translated as 'combustible, vulnerable, expendable'. If only we'd known.

The early CVEs had a top speed never much more than 12 knots, and carried only a dozen or so aircraft, but they protected convoy after convoy.

I remember seeing a brass plate displayed at the head of our ship's gangway:[2]

> This is the first ship to be built by the
> Portland (Oregon) Agricultural Machinery Company.
> May God bless all who sail in her.

*

It took us three days over New Year 1942/3 to fly back north to Macrihanish, with various bits of squadron gear lashed to the

Swordfish bomb-racks under the wings, including a ladder and my bicycle. In mid-flight over the lowlands I watched in fascination as a pedal unwound itself from the bicycle and spun away earthward into somebody's back garden.

We landed halfway, staying at an airfield outside Sunderland, otherwise occupied by a squadron of Spitfires flown by Poles. It was time for a party, and as midnight approached, the drink was flowing freely. I told the Polish pilots that I would like to wish their commander – a colonel – a Happy New Year in Polish. Eagerly they taught me to say two phrases that they swore were the common Polish salutations for such occasions. I can only remember them phonetically as: 'Hochka hoynya!' and 'Ti stari biccu!'

When the bells struck, I strode up to the Colonel, clicked my heels and raised my glass and gave my salutation. I should have known better – especially as, from the corner of my eye, I could see the Polish pilots writhing in laughter. The Colonel's eyes nearly popped out of his head; what I had said was on the lines of 'Come on in, big boy!' (as from a prostitute in a doorway), and 'You stupid slab of beef!' (when the offer is declined).

At Macrihanish we waited for word of HMS *Dasher*. It was realized that, for all the practice on the dummy strip at Arbroath, only two of our pilots had ever actually landed on a ship's deck. The rest were sent off to learn how to do it, putting down on the ancient HMS *Argus*, a venerable (1917) ship that featured something rather remarkable: a retractable bridge in the middle of the flight deck, that would be lowered when aircraft were being flown if anyone remembered in time. Three successful deck landings on *Argus* qualified my pilot Bobby as an expert. A week later, we flew to Scapa Flow in the Orkneys, and landed the whole squadron on *Dasher*.

In all the excitement, and amongst all the satisfaction of finally becoming ship-borne, still I was apprehensive. For all its dangers, for all the anti-aircraft fire and balloons and Me109s, the south coast had some things going for it. Thorney Island was solid ground. My wife, my home had been there in a small cottage by the airfield. Between operations, we could sleep out of danger. Aircraft carriers never ceased to be dangerous, either by day or by night. They were targets; U-boats sent torpedoes at them in the small hours while we dozed, battleships fired guns at them, the *Luftwaffe* dropped bombs on them; in due course Japanese kamikazes would dive straight into them. They were slow, big and vulnerable. HMS *Glorious* had been caught virtually defenceless by *Scharnhorst* and *Gneisenau* and destroyed; then *Ark Royal* was sunk with a single torpedo. *Courageous* needed two torpedoes, but took 518 men and two Swordfish squadrons down with her. The Germans did not have aircraft carriers, and one could not help wondering why.[3]

HMS *Dasher* was hardly a vessel to inspire confidence. She was a curious thing to look at; the wooden flight deck was built on scaffolding above the cargo deck, like a trellis table. From the side you could see straight underneath it; at the time, it reminded me of a waiter holding a tray of drinks up on his fingers, but looking at pictures of her today makes me think of an elongated oil-rig. A tiny, cramped little open bridge clung to her starboard side, as though stuck on by mistake. There was a 400-foot flight deck and a single aircraft lift, and the hangar below was so small as to make it impossible to range aircraft quickly; in all but severe weather, at least some were kept up on the flight deck.

She was never a healthy ship – and from the crew we began to pick up fragments of her story that hardly increased our confidence. Converted from an American merchantman (called *Rio de Janeiro*) into a carrier in just three months, things went wrong from the outset. The first time the diesel engines were started, they blew up. During her initial trials on the Hudson River, she ran aground. Throughout her brief career, the twin engines failed again and again; she never did dash very fast. Often the motors would not start, but backfired like an old motorbike. Of the first four aircraft to land on her – Swordfish of 837 Squadron – one went over the side. No sooner had she reached Britain than it was decided that her flight deck was not long enough, so she went into dock on the Clyde to have it lengthened by some forty feet.

In October 1942, carrying Swordfish and Sea Hurricanes, she sailed to the Mediterranean together with the antique *Argus* to escort Operation *Torch*, the North African landings against the

Vichy French. On the return journey (15 November) *Dasher*'s sister ship *Avenger* was hit by a single torpedo, blew up and sank.

Still *Dasher*'s engines were giving trouble, both on the outward and the return journeys, so she was sent to Liverpool for yet more work. Finally, after taking a battering from the sea in the Minch, *Dasher* reached Scapa Flow – and we landed on her and explored.

If we had thought conditions at Macrihanish were spartan, the cramped quarters on *Dasher* were extraordinary; as a merchantman, she'd been built for a crew of fewer than forty men, and now carried more than five hundred, packed into compartments that had begun life as freight holds. At least, though, she was new; there was a soda fountain – she was, of course, an American ship. The officers' cabins were above the engine room and the exhaust piping rose up between them before ducking out under the side; some of the cabins were nicely warmed.

There was even provision for projecting films, though my *Manual of Seamanship* had something to say about that, for the old celluloid film stock was highly flammable:

> Most ships now carry a cinematograph apparatus. A routine for showing the films should be made out. Precautions must be observed to guard against fire. Displays should take place on the upper deck, and on no account near any explosives. Celluloid films should not be allowed on board unless in well-fitting iron boxes and only one film should be out of its box at a time.[4]

We found that we were a rather fragmented flying company. Along with the six 816 Squadron Swordfish, there were three others from another squadron, together with a flight of Hurricanes from yet another fitted with arrestor hooks for deck landing and with strengthened undercarriage, and now rather grandly re-named Sea Hurricanes. Still, they were not true carrier aircraft; their wings could not fold, and they spent most of their lives up on deck to avoid cluttering the hangar. Each group brought their own fitters along with their aircrew; the ship was crowded, confused and cross. One Duty Flying Officer – Brian Bennett – was called on to range two 816 Squadron Swordfish for a patrol: it took half an hour to get them from the hangar up onto the flight deck, and Brian was tersely ordered to submit an explanation for this in writing – but the explanation was simple enough: 816 Squadron's aircraft were at the back of the hangar, and he had had to find the handling crews for the other squadrons' aircraft and get them to shuffle their charges out of the way first. (Not long after this, composite squadrons became the norm so that, for instance, on HMS *Tracker* 816 was the only squadron aboard, with a mix of Swordfish and Seafires under one command.)

At the very end of January 1943, we sailed for Loch Ewe, a sea-loch in north-west Scotland. Loch Ewe had been hastily prepared as a naval base early in the war, because Scapa Flow was supposedly vulnerable to German bombers from Norway. Loch Ewe was deep enough to accommodate the largest ships, gave immediate access to the open Atlantic, and was well-sheltered.[5] Having been nothing but a small fishing community, Loch Ewe suddenly became the main rendezvous for convoys on the Arctic route to Murmansk, as well as many of those crossing the North Atlantic. The loch was very isolated, a long, hard drive on narrow roads from anywhere, but surrounded by astonishingly beautiful mountain scenery – and, in 1943, by anti-aircraft batteries and barrage balloons. Across the mouth of the loch were torpedo nets, while on the seabed lay thick cables forming a magnetic loop; if a submarine slunk in over this underwater, a needle would swing on a meter on the shore and the operator could trigger a line of depth charges. For all this, one felt grateful; one would have felt even more secure if HMS *Nelson* had not hit a mine right in the entrance to the loch.

From early 1942 onwards, huge numbers of merchant ships and their naval escorts had assembled here, packed with Mathilda and Valentine tanks, diesel engines, field guns and tractors for the defence of Russia,[6] more than four millions tons of supplies. *Dasher* joined convoy JW53, a large convoy heading for Murmansk.

Even as a sub-lieutenant, I knew well enough what could happen to these convoys if the submarines found us before we detected them. A few months beforehand, the infamous convoy PQ17 had made the dreadful error of scattering, and the ships had been picked off one by one; twenty-nine out of thirty-four had gone down. Three months later, PQ18 had lost thirteen out of forty-four vessels. No one, seaman or airman, swimming in that sea would last long. Water is an excellent conductor of heat, and we would be sailing within sight of the Arctic ice; a man swimming in the Barents Sea has the bodily warmth sucked out of him in moments.

So, the convoy's aircraft and escorts would fight to keep the submarines and the bombers off. On the first leg to Iceland we had three destroyers, with corvettes, minesweepers, even an armed trawler to protect us. From Iceland onwards there would be a whole swarm of destroyers, minesweepers and 'Flower'-class corvettes – *Matchless*, *Musketeer*, *Bryony*, *Bergamot*, *Poppy* and *Jason*, *Bluebell* and *Camellia* and others, thirteen in all – with the cruisers *Belfast*, *Sheffield* and *Cumberland*, and the battleships *Howe* and *King George V* in the background in case any German capital ship headed for the convoy. But none of this would do *Dasher* any good. What did for us was the weather.

On the trip to Iceland, the storms began. After several days of hurricane force winds, we had to seek shelter with two of the cruisers in Akureyi fjord, while the rest of the convoy skulked nearby in Seydisfjord; neither was a place for shore leave, being surrounded by snowy mountainous wastelands down to the water's edge. I've a photo of a group of us on *Dasher*'s flight deck in the snow, perhaps apprehensive as to what flying conditions would be like in the next few days (*plate 4*).

When at last the weather improved, together we set off for Murmansk in Kola Inlet around North Cape. For twenty-four hours all went well enough, the weather was fair, the sea was calm. We swept the snow off the flight deck and flew our first anti-submarine patrols – the first that 816 Squadron had ever flown. We suddenly felt rather important, although made sharply conscious of how cold in our open cockpits we were going to be.

But that was the end of our flying. That evening the barometer plummeted; at midnight, the wind-speed indicator on the bridge was reading 90 knots and then went off the dial altogether. Everyone went below; the bridge shut down. The storms were back.

Almost at once, three merchantmen turned about for Scapa Flow, fearful of losing their cargoes off the deck. The rest of the convoy put their bows to the wind and waited.

But the winds did not diminish, and the sea got up fearfully. More ships turned around, one of them the cruiser *Sheffield*, which lost the armoured roof of its forward gun turret, ripped off by a pounding sea. *Dasher* pitched and rolled like a drunk; there was no question of flying now, with the high flight deck waving about like a flag in the wind. It was difficult enough to remain on one's feet even below amongst the bulkheads and piping, but the hangar had become thoroughly dangerous: Swordfish began slithering about, snapped wires lashing and heavy tools smashing into men and aircraft. We were told to clear out.

Up above it was far worse; even attempting to walk across the wooden flight deck would be a suicidal venture. The three Sea Hurricanes still up there (because their wings couldn't fold for storage) began to break loose of their lashing wires, sliding back and forth, threatening to sweep each other and the rest of us over the side. Finally, one of the aircraft had to be freed and pushed overboard, before it did any more damage. By the next morning, the other two had disappeared.

The crew were ordered to stay below, and did not need told twice. Many of us began to wonder if *Dasher* could stay upright. We fell quiet.

Dasher could not take such treatment. She'd been cheaply and quickly welded, built for pottering up and down the US seaboard, not for this. She was not strong enough. One of the 816 Squadron ratings went up to the bridge and asked if it was all right that they could see the sea through their mess-deck bulkhead. When an officer was sent below to inspect the damage, he found a sixty-foot split in the hull close to the waterline. The ship's steel plating was breaking open and she had begun to take in water.

Ignominiously, we had to turn about and return to Scapa Flow for repairs, leaving the convoy without air cover. In the event, they all survived without us, although beset by U-boats. The gaggle of destroyers hurried about seeing off the submarines, while the weather and the ferocity of the anti-aircraft fire kept off the bombers. The whole convoy reached Murmansk – but on the return, one of the merchantmen began to break up as we had done, her welding coming apart also, until she foundered.

Dasher crept back into Scapa Flow with her tail between her legs. After emergency patching, she headed for Dundee for proper repairs escorted by a destroyer, while 816 Squadron flew ashore to Hatston in the Orkneys to await her return. There, we found that we had coincided with a visit to the Home Fleet by His Majesty King George VI. We felt less than glorious. A single Swordfish was mustered for inspection, the pilot – Brian Bennett again – paraded beside it with his aircrew. I have a photo of them (*plate 5*): Brian is starting to raise his hand to salute as the King and a clutch of admirals approach, their forearms weighed down with gold trimmings. Behind Brian's Swordfish, an old pusher-prop Walrus and an Albacore can be seen. Three obsolete biplanes: what a display of sea power.

Three weeks later, *Dasher* was back in the Clyde; we flew down to meet her. We knew now what our next assignment would be: we were to escort a convoy from the Western Approaches across the Atlantic to Halifax, Nova Scotia. But this time, *Dasher* barely left the Clyde.

It was shortly before we were due to sail, having spent a few days in the Irish Sea on trials and exercises. All seemed well. We were in the wardroom having a drink before dinner when one of the signals ratings entered and asked the steward which one was me; he then handed me a signal. It was from my sister-in-law, telling me that my mother had had a severe stroke and was dying. The Commander and Ralph Stallard-Penoyre, the Squadron CO, were both there in the wardroom; so too was my pilot, Bobby Creighton. I was obviously very agitated. I told them what had happened, and showed them the telegram. Was there any possibility of my getting down to see her?

There were discussions – but later that evening I was told that I'd been granted forty-eight hours' compassionate leave, under strict orders to get back before we sailed. Everyone put themselves out to help. The 'Pay-bob' opened his office to issue a travel warrant (I had very little money on board) and a boat was found to take me ashore to Gourock. I caught a night sleeper from Glasgow to

Euston, and finally reached my parents' home at Harpenden in Hertfordshire around midday, very bleary-eyed.

My mother was lying peacefully in bed, but was exceedingly frail. The GP lived a few doors away; he told me that she had only days to live. I asked: would he mind if I sought a second opinion? No, he had no objection – but after he had given me details of her medical history and her heart condition, and after I had talked to my father, I realized that there was no point in interfering. I sat with her for as long as I could, and after a while she took my hand and smiled faintly, whispering:

'You've been a good son to me, Bob.'

It was a beautiful, sunny afternoon. After feeding her a little lunch, I was able to carry her downstairs in my arms and to lay her on a couch that my sisters had placed out in the garden. It was the last time she was to feel the sun on her face, and the last time that I saw her.

That night, I caught a sleeper from Euston back up to Glasgow, and then in the grey dawn light the local train back along the Clyde to Gourock. As we jogged along that last leg, a couple of lads in the carriage began to speak of some serious naval calamity in the Clyde that they had heard rumour of.

There was a landing-stage near Gourock for the boats from the Fleet ships anchored there. I made my way there and asked the Chief Petty Officer in charge if he expected any boat from *Dasher*. He looked at me suspiciously, and gave a rather surprising answer.

'Why d'you want to know?'

'I have to get back on board. It's my ship.'

'You'd better go along to the Duty Officer,' he said. 'They've given him a room in the Wrens' quarters for the time being. He'll tell you what he can. *Dasher* blew up and sank in mid-stream yesterday afternoon. She went down in a few minutes. I don't know any details.'

I suppose I must have stared at him. Completely bewildered, I made my way along to the Wrennery.

My memories of the days that followed immediately are scant; some sort of protective shock mechanism set in, shielding me from the loss of so many of my friends and companions. I can remember meeting one or two of the surviving pilots and observers and hearing their individual stories. Nobody knew why the ship had blown up. They had been testing *Dasher*'s engines out in the waters south of Little Cumbrae island. Some of the 816 Squadron Swordfish and Sea Hurricanes were still ashore at Macrihanish, due to return to the ship the following day; others had been flying, and had just landed on; they'd been taken down in the lift for refuelling and maintenance in the hangar below...

There had been a tremendous explosion, so powerful that the aircraft lift – an object weighing sixty tons – had been thrown high into the air and over the side. Filled with fires and with a large hole blasted in her stern, the ship began to sink very rapidly, going down in less than eight minutes. Those of the crew who were below decks went straight down with her, but a number managed to get into the water, where they faced a new peril: as *Dasher* sank, large quantities of aviation fuel were released from her tanks, which now came bubbling to the surface and ignited all around the men.

Brian Bennett made it into the water. He told me afterwards that it had all been so fast that there had been no time to understand what was happening. Brian and a group of aircrew were relaxing in the wardroom with a cup of tea when of a sudden there was a strange *thump* noise. The lights in the wardroom failed, and everything became creepily still: none of the usual mechanical sounds or vibrations. They groped their way from the wardroom to the Aircrew Ready Room, grabbing their Mae West life jackets in passing. Brian and his observer, Flight Sergeant Alex Grieve, hurried up onto the flight deck. Looking back along the deck, they saw smoke and then fire pouring out of the lift shaft. As they looked, the ship lurched; *Dasher* began to go down by the stern at an ever-more alarming tilt. They crossed the flight deck, but as they went the slope increased so rapidly that before they were halfway across they were forced to go crabwise on hands and knees. Now they were hurrying for the catwalk along the side of the flight deck; before they got there, two Sea Hurricanes broke free and rolled past them, and down into the water.

They reached the catwalk, which had become more like a ladder. Brian and Sergeant Grieves climbed forward to the bow, which was pointing into the air. Many of the ship's company were up there, leaping into the water. Brian and Grieves clung on as *Dasher* began to sink rapidly by the stern. At some point he could not recall, Brian saw Grieves jumping; he never saw him again. Brian let the ship carry him downwards, and then floated off in the sea. He said that the last he'd seen of *Dasher* was her bow disappearing by his shoulder.

This had only taken eight minutes. Now black smoke began to appear on the water round him, and soon the sea was coated with burning aviation fuel. Brian managed to swim around the fires and – almost half an hour later – was picked out of the exceedingly cold sea by a boat from some ship that had hurried to help.

But he was very lucky. All around him, men were either burned to death or were dying of hypothermia; although there were two civilian freighters nearby that rushed to help, for most they were too late. Of the ship's total company of 528, there were 379 dead in a few minutes.

Among our aircrew, the class distinction held: few of the 816 Squadron officers had died, because fortunately many of the aircraft had been on shore; there were two Hurricanes and six Swordfish in the hangar at the time of the explosion, with two Swordfish on deck. But aircrew tended to stay higher in the ship, near the Ready Room and Operations Room if not out on the flight deck, and so were not caught in the inferno below, or trapped or drowned. Just two pilots and one observer were lost. Of our air gunners and telegraphists, however, our 'Acting Leading Airmen', a number were gone. But the heaviest casualties were among our ground crew, our riggers. The Air Mechanics (2nd Class), the Air Fitters (ordinary), the Air Artificers and Leading Radio Mechanics (Air) – of the crowd of these, our squadron troops, people we knew well and trusted implicitly to keep our aircraft fit for flying and our lives safe, only seven had survived, for the rest had been in the heart of the ship, eating in the deep crew mess, or working in the hangar.

We had also lost our Commanding Officer, Ralph Stallard-Penoyre. He had only been with us the few months since Olly Patch had been dismissed. A Royal Navy officer in a squadron now almost entirely RNVR, we had never got to know Ralph well. He had given me the leave to go to my dying mother, and perhaps because of that I was still alive.

*

The forlorn attempts at salvage and recovery began. We were all sent on 'survivor's leave' for two weeks. I, at least, had my wife. My mother had died a few days after my visit, and I was able to go to her funeral; she was buried alongside her beloved firstborn son Bert in Eltham churchyard, and some of our old neighbours from Martin Bowes Road came.

Very little news reached me of survivors from *Dasher*, though I knew already that one of my closest friends had drowned. At the end of two weeks we were instructed to report back – yet again – to RNAS Daedalus at Lee-on-Solent, where I found to my great relief that my pilot Bobby Creighton was alive, and that I would be flying with him once more. He had been on board *Dasher* at the time of the explosion, in our cabin. When the lights of the sinking ship failed, he had been unable to find his Mae West survival jacket in the darkness but, knowing me to be on shore, he had taken mine.

The naval authorities, meanwhile, were frantically trying to work out what had happened, appalled by the possibility of sabotage or perhaps of U-boats penetrating the hitherto 'safe' waters of the Clyde approaches. So they suppressed all reports of the accident, a blanket ban being placed on any discussion of what had occurred. One pilot who had been circling overhead at the time of the accident, who had seen with his own eyes the explosion, the lift being tossed high in the air and bodies thrown off it into the sea, was told by a Navy desk officer in London that he was mistaken, that he had seen nothing of the sort, and should shut up and wait for further instructions.

The families of my dead friends were told nothing. They received a derisory telegram from the Casualty Section of the Navy, which gave the following reassurances:

Death was due to explosion on board. Ship was in company with other vessels. Full medical assistance was available immediately. Everything that could be done to save lives and mitigate suffering was done.

That was it. Three days later, the Casualty Section wrote to the Admiralty complaining that they could not fob off families in this way, and saying:

Casualty staff are having a difficult time with relatives on the present meagre information.

Meanwhile, the hastily convened board of inquiry was taking evidence from the survivors. The board consisted of five senior commanders, including those from *Dasher's* sister ship HMS *Archer*, who certainly did not want the same thing happening to their command. The explosion, they were told, had come from the vicinity of the depth charge store and the aircraft petrol store, but the sound of the explosion – more of a deep *whump* than a sharp crack – persuaded them that it had been petrol, not high explosives, that had detonated. People began to pick holes in *Dasher's* American construction and conversion, which had, of course, been undertaken at great speed: the lighting below decks, for instance, was considered sub-standard, such that a spark from a light switch could have ignited petrol vapour. The board reached a conclusion that rubbed in the banality of the disaster:

We are of the opinion that … there may have been an accumulation of petrol vapour in the main petrol compartment and that this could have been ignited by a man smoking in the shaft tunnel, or through someone dropping a cigarette down from the Fleet Air Arm mess deck to the petrol control compartment or below.

So it could even have been one of my friends in 816 Squadron that caused it, with a fag end.

There was another curious aftermath to the disaster. At almost exactly this time, one of the most famous deceptions of the war – Operation *Mincemeat* – was launched, to deceive the Germans into thinking that, rather than invade Sicily, the Allies were about to land in Greece. Operation *Mincement* required there to be a fake Naval intelligence officer, Major William Martin of the Royal Marines, whose dead body would be found in the sea off Portugal, and who would be carrying documents that suggested a forthcoming landing in Greece. The plan all worked wonderfully well, but there has been a question hovering over it ever since: whose was the corpse that was used as 'Major Martin'? For some time, the evidence had pointed to a Welsh tramp, Glyndwr Michael, who had been found dead in London, apparently as a result of eating rat poison.

But in the 1990s a former policeman called Colin Gibbon raised doubts: surely, he argued, any competent forensics doctor (whether German, Portuguese or Spanish) performing a post-mortem on 'Major Martin' would be able to tell the difference between death by drowning and death by warfarin. Furthermore, was it likely that the body of an alcoholic Welsh down-and-out would pass muster as a fit and healthy thirty-six-year-old major of Marines?

Gibbon came up with a better idea. The body was not the tramp's, but one of the many lost on HMS *Dasher*. It had, he decided, been collected by a submarine – HMS *Seraph* – and whisked away for use as Mincemeat.[7]

It was just the sort of conspiracy to delight armchair historians, but it left me with mixed feelings. What an undignified end that would have been, to be dressed up as someone else, dumped in the sea and used as a trick, and at last to be finally buried under the wrong name in a cemetery in Spain. But then, why not? Bertrand Russell said: 'I believe that when I die, I rot.' As it was, the deaths of my friends had been quite pointless; at least one of them might have been useful thereafter.

It took me a long time to shed the emotions of those weeks: too much, too personal and all at once, compounded by my mother's death, the guilt of the survivor, and a stupid feeling of resentment – for, amongst everything else that had gone down with *Dasher* were my flying logbooks, my bicycle, and a treasured antique snuff-horn.

*

We had to put ourselves back together. As the investigations into the *Dasher* proceeded, at Lee-on-Solent 816 Squadron was rebuilt. But another carrier had to be made ready for us. One consequence of the disaster, and the very secretive inquiry into what had happened, was alarm regarding inadequate safety provision for fuel and ammunition storage – and the consequence of that was delay, as similar ships were modified.

We, meanwhile, needed a new Commanding Officer, and Lieutenant Pete Pryor (RN) stood in for two months. We also needed some replacement aircrew. Most of all, however, we needed new ground crew, only seven of our eighty having survived *Dasher*. We were bereaved.

We had, as a squadron, one other focus for affection: our dogs. Officer aircrew were billeted in a building called the *White House*, a sizeable private home that had been absorbed into the Daedalus aerodrome by recurrent extensions of the runways. Here the observers and pilots lived together; it was a companionable slum, and improved by dogs. Judy was a Great Dane bitch, owned by an observer, Ken Horsfield. She was vast, almost large enough to ride. Bruce approximated to a Labrador; he materialized from somewhere and moved in with us. One morning, when most of us were out flying, 'Captain's rounds' arrived for an inspection, and went upstairs; there, Judy and Bruce were dozing peaceably on the beds. Waking to see familiar uniforms, they bounded about in welcome thinking it must be time for walks, food or play, the colossal Judy pursuing the visitors outside.

There followed a confrontation.

'Who gave permission for the keeping of dogs on station?'

'No one, sir.'

'Who is in charge of those animals?'

'No one really, sir.'

'Right. I want them both off the base by morning.'

This deadline was extended to forty-eight hours when Ken Horsfield protested that Judy was a delicate and valuable pedigree bitch. But the dogs had to go, and things looked dark – until just then the order came for the squadron to move; we were going to the West Country. Bruce was found lodgings at the nearby pub, while Judy (after we'd regretfully dropped a scheme to fly her to Devon dressed as an air gunner) travelled with the ground crew by train. We contrived to leave grubby paw-prints on the White House ceiling, as a parting gesture.

*

In May 1943, while we waited for a new ship, the squadron moved to RAF Exeter, a Coastal Command station (now the city airport), which was under the command of a short-tempered and hard-drinking RN Lieutenant-Commander known as 'Shaggers' Whitworth; he disapproved of wives haunting air stations, thinking them a debilitating distraction, and was heard to pronounce loudly 'You can't fight *and* fuck!' This was not calculated to improve the morale of a devastated squadron. It was our wives and girlfriends that kept us sane.

Nobody loved Shaggers. When he eventually left us in June, Brian Bennett claimed that Shaggers had stolen all his clean shirts and socks and had taken them with him.

We began training flights once more. For a brief while, being land-based again seemed safer than the idea of a new ship. We now had six new black Swordfish Mk IIs for night flying, something we were supposedly expert at. We were to practise a novel set of skills: chasing and bombing German fast torpedo E-boats. Slowly – more than a year in advance – preparations for the long-planned invasion of France were beginning in the Channel ports; the Germans had a good idea what was coming and were trying everything they could to disrupt these preparations, including sending E-boats in among Allied shipping – a reckless and courageous thing to do, very much in the spirit of the bravery of the U-boats. The E-boats attacked at night; we were supposed to stop them. Special bombs had been designed for the purpose of sinking E-boats; they were intended to plunge down below the boats and come up to explode against their lightly armoured underside. We spent happy hours practising 'glide bombing' – the required technique – in broad daylight on the bombing range at Teignmouth, and at night chasing the E-boats that used to invade Lyme Bay. I don't think that we ever sank one; perhaps we scared them off. There was something absurd about countering high-speed E-boats with – of all aircraft – the 80-knot Swordfish. If the wind was against us, the E-boats were almost as fast as we were, and we could pursue them across the sea half the night, chasing their moonlit wakes without catching up.

Glide bombing, though, was curiously delightful. The idea was to creep up on the E-boats without letting them hear our approach. We would be directed to the targets by shore radar at Start Point. As we approached, we would throttle the big Pegasus engine right back and drift down from astern so quietly that one could hear the wind in the struts and wires, fluttering towards the wake of the target – for this tactic, at least, the immensely air-stable Swordfish was ideal – to plop the bomb into the water. If nothing else, it gave the crews of the practice target boats a fright. To perform the trick, the 816 Squadron Swordfish had to be equipped with cutting edge technology unheard of in the old biplanes: radio. No longer would we have to unwind yards of aerial weighted down with bits of lead to flap around in the sky behind us while we tapped out Morse. No longer would we have to communicate with other aircraft by 'zogging' (hand signals) or a flickering Aldis lamp (which would have been seen by the E-boat, giving the attack away). Now we could gossip happily with our fellows in the air while chasing intruders – at least, in theory. Unfortunately, *en route* to Exeter something seemed to be very wrong with our new radios. Strange voices and frightening commands were being given, concerning something we didn't understand at all, something alarming, something about fighter aircraft coming our way, about evasive action, about opening fire… Only at last did we work out that we had become involved in an RAF fighter sortie over northern France. We had been issued with tuning crystals for the wrong wavelength.

*

There was almost a holiday feel, with Devon seaside pleasures; sometimes we could get down to the beach and enjoy excellent swimming. Three of the squadron rented a house near the aerodrome and installed their wives there. They called it 'Lech Cottage'. Shaggers Whitworth learned of the house and its name and demanded to know the reason for both, clearly suspecting that bedroom activities detrimental to flying duty were taking place. One of the pilots claimed it was from the Polish name 'Lech'.

For the Poles had arrived at Exeter before us, a fighter squadron of Spitfires, which the Polish and Czech pilots flew with extraordinary flair and ruthlessness. One reason they flew so ferociously well was that in Poland they had trained on – and already fought the *Luftwaffe* with – antiquated biplane aircraft. We could on occasion see them eyeing our Swordfish with something like understanding and affection. One of the Poles was a poster artist of ability who painted a grand and vibrant mural around the walls and the serving hatch of the officers' mess (*plate 6*): it depicted a line of long-legged lovelies in bathing suits with feathers attached to their backsides, surrounded by desperate flocks of airmen – some scampering across the tarmac, others in Spitfires – and the whole surmounted by the words 'Good Health' in half a dozen languages: *Na zdravi! Kia ora!*

*

When at last we got our own commander again, he was just the man to put the battered and demoralized squadron together again. He was a very different character from Shaggers. Our new boss was Lieutenant Commander Freddie Nottingham, RNVR, DSC, an outgoing and gregarious man. He was a South African with no love of formality or hierarchy, who in civilian life ran a peach farm near Johannesburg.

Freddie Nottingham had acquired a civilian pilot's licence in South Africa, and had volunteered for the FAA as far back as February 1939, when few people thought of it as a glamorous career choice. He had survived a succession of desperate missions: he had been with 825 Squadron during the Dunkirk evacuation when the Swordfish had supported the Army as best they could, his squadron losing eight out of its twelve aircraft. He had flown Albacores (the 'modernized' Swordfish) with 829 Squadron from HMS *Formidable* at the Battle of Matapan, a famous victory over the Italian fleet, but soon afterwards *Formidable* was seriously damaged by German bombers off Crete. Freddie was next sent to 830 Squadron at the shattered airfield of Hal Far in Malta from where, in spite of there being hardly a building at the aerodrome not reduced to rubble, still the Swordfish doggedly laid mines in Tripoli harbour and attacked convoys sailing to supply the *Afrika Korps*. They flew every night. One of Freddie's torpedoes had sunk a 13,000-ton Italian merchantman, though his aircraft had been badly damaged and he'd flown back to the carrier with fire licking around his fuel tank. For his leadership he'd won a DSC. After Hal Far, he had been sent to Ceylon as senior pilot with 815 Squadron on *Hermes*, but the carrier had been sunk by Japanese dive-bombers. Next it was 827 Squadron on *Indomitable* to Madagascar, and at last to us and 816 Squadron chasing E-boats and submarines.

Freddie was to be with us until the following spring. When he eventually left 816 Squadron, he continued his adventures in the Pacific, commanding 854 Squadron flying Grumman Avengers from HMS *Illustrious*. He later told me how, on a bombing mission in the last weeks of the war, his port wing had been shot off by Japanese flak and his aircraft had spiralled into the sea. His two crewmen had been killed but, as usual, Freddie had survived. As he bobbed in the water, to his astonishment an American submarine, the *Kingfisher*, had appeared nearby. The duty officer had flung open the hatch and yelled: 'Hey, Limey, come in out of the wet!'

Freddie Nottingham survived them all; he was just what we needed.

He was famous among us for his battle cry: 'Fly with me, my boys, and you'll live to see your grandchildren!' – which, for most of us, was true. He had little time for service protocol. A childhood accident falling off a horse had injured his right arm, so that he was unable to salute in the prescribed manner, and he played on this cheerfully.

When Freddy got married, his bride Lois was a Wren from the stockbroker belt in Surrey. A number of us went to the reception at her father's house. Here, Freddie quickly wearied of standing in line shaking hands with the well-heeled financiers he had inherited along with his new wife, and he slipped away to an upstairs room. He whistled down to me from a bedroom window: 'Hey, Bobby! Come up here, and fetch a bottle of wine. Bring the others!'

Moments later we were all playing poker dice. But then the door crashed open and a furious Lois roared at him: 'Freddy – get downstairs!'

In June 1943, it was enough for us that he was both cheerful and decisive. He was an excellent leader, and he needed to be. We were putting *Dasher* behind us now, and were assigned to a new aircraft carrier, HMS *Tracker*, and to the North Atlantic.

Notes

1. The *Hanover* was captured near Jamaica in March 1940. In mid-1941 she re-appeared as HMS *Audacity* with a flight deck but no lift or hangar, so that her six Wildcat fighters lived permanently on deck. For the aircrew, living conditions were luxurious, including the old first-class cabins with *en suite* bath.

2. Robert's memoir states that he saw this plate on HMS *Dasher*, but online records agree that *Dasher* was built by the Sun Shipbuilding Co. of Chester, Penn., while Robert's other ships – *Tracker* and *Chaser* – were built by Seattle-Tacoma and Ingalls respectively, with further companies doing the conversion work. I have not been able to establish what it was that the Agricultural Machinery Co. built; possibly they did pre-fabricate hull sections that the dockyards later assembled.

3. The German lack of carriers was largely a result of inter-service rivalry and suspicion. One large ship – the *Graf Zeppelin* – was built but was never completed, and her captured hulk ended up being used for target practice by the Russians.

4. Cinema fires were not uncommon and were often fatal to projectionists, as Robert's father would have known. J & N Steele's *The Secrets of HMS Dasher* includes a cut-away plan of a ship of the same class, showing the cinema equipment stowed next door to the hangar.

5. Many traces of the defence installations may be seen in the environs of Loch Ewe today. Although at the same latitude as Moscow, the climate here is so benign that at the head of the loch are the gardens of Inverewe, begun in the 1860s and famous for the extraordinary collection of plants from far warmer homes, including bamboos and azaleas.

6. The real strategic value of these convoys is much debated; the Russians had (for example) no very high opinion of British light tanks, and would have much preferred American types. But politically, it was essential for the Allies to be seen to be supporting the Soviet Union in any way possible. The cost – in terms of ships sunk, lives and supplies lost – was much higher on the Arctic convoys than in the North Atlantic.

7. This is the theory advanced in J & N Steele's book, *The Secrets of HMS Dasher* (2002), which I discussed with Robert. See the note on this in the Introduction, p.10. I have reconstructed this passage from later conversations.

CHAPTER FIVE
Tracker in the Storms

Tracker was a 'Woolworth ship' – another hurriedly improvised US carrier, with the same expanse of Oregon pine decking fitted above her superstructure. This news filled us initially with quiet dread, for the *Dasher* explosion had still never been satisfactorily explained to us.

But *Tracker* was more ambitious, built from scratch and better designed than *Dasher's* primitive conversion. She was more comfortable in every respect, and ran more smoothly too; instead of unreliable and juddering diesel engines, she had twin steam turbines, giving her a speed of almost 18 knots. *Tracker* was no larger than *Dasher* – her 480-foot flight deck almost exactly the same length – but she was far better organized. She had a full-length hangar and lifts fore and aft, which meant that sorting and ranging aircraft was much easier, although even so there were times when the only aircraft available would belong to some other aircrew who were resting, so that one might find oneself in a 'strange' machine. Every aircraft had its own little ways and habits (the trim sometimes corrected by sticking weights on the tailplane), so this was not what one wanted when flying over a besieged North Atlantic or Arctic convoy.

No. 816 Squadron was now combined with a flight of Seafire fighters: the old error of multiple squadrons mixed up on one carrier had been understood. We were *Tracker's* first squadron and for most of our new aircrew, she was their first carrier; many of them would be learning the difficult arts of flying-off and landing-on not from the luxurious length of a great fleet carrier like *Ark Royal* or *Illustrious* but from a tiny wobbling bit of planking – what Brian would describe as 'a gyrating cricket pitch'. (Brian did not make this any easier for himself, landing on *Tracker* with four bicycles lashed to the rocket racks, two under each wing of his ever-forgiving Swordfish).

Thus, as we awaited our first convoy, a new task fell to me: of preparing a compilation of film shots to illustrate the finer points of placing a Swordfish onto a heaving carrier deck in heavy seas. Deck landing in the shelter of the Clyde was fairly easy, but there were always new problems. No. 816 Squadron's Swordfish were armed with eight anti-submarine rockets mounted on racks under the lower wing (the doped canvas here prudently replaced with metal sheeting). These were wonderfully effective weapons, but they were also alarmingly heavy. If the pilot came down too heavily, even the sturdy Swordfish undercarriage would spread out sideways like a monstrous ballet dancer. Then the huge propeller would bite suddenly into the decking, causing the engine to slam to a halt, probably with internal damage as a result.

If a Swordfish flopped down like this, the next problem was moving it aside rapidly, for there could be further aircraft lining up behind it to land also. The end of a mission often coincided with the end of the day, with fuel perhaps down to dangerously low levels, and with the light fading; no one wanted to be deck landing in the dark if they could help it, certainly not in heavy seas. *Tracker* did have deck lights but they were feeble blue things, easily obscured in bad weather – and, whatever the weather had been like when you took off, there was no saying what it might be hours later. To move a damaged aircraft off the middle of the flight deck quickly was imperative. Part of the solution was a simple innovation: no one could agree on who first thought of it. The riggers fitted a short length of ½-inch steel cable between the legs of the undercarriage, which with luck would prevent the undercarriage from collapsing in a heavy landing, allowing the deck hands to jab a fork lift in under the fuselage, to lift the aircraft aside. We were rather pleased with our brainchild and were mystified when our attempts to inform the rest of the fleet of our ingenuity met with a frigid lack of interest; they could not understand why we were smashing up the aircraft in the first place.

All these things we fretted over while working up *Tracker* on the Clyde – not a place of happy memories: we were very near the location where *Dasher* had blown apart. We lost aircraft even now: a Swordfish, trying to land-on in poor visibility, misjudged its approach and went over the side, with the loss of two aircrew. But again, after just three decent landings on a virtually stationary carrier deck, our new pilots were deemed to be ready for the high seas.

Together with our ten Swordfish, we carried half a dozen Seafires to provide air defence against enemy bombers attacking convoys. The Seafires were as fast and agile as their progenitor the Spitfire, but in 1943 they did not yet have folding wings, making them a thorough nuisance on a small carrier. Nor was their undercarriage (although adapted for carrier use) anything like robust enough for the tumult of the North Atlantic; the slightest bump on landing, and the wheels snapped off, sending the Seafire slithering helplessly into other parked aircraft and any riggers who happened to be in the way. So it was the seemingly indestructible Swordfish that would be flown in all weathers, while the Seafires were to be kept parked out of the way like pampered racehorses, only allowed to go galloping when the sun shined – or when enemy aircraft were sighted.

*

In the meantime, as we prepared our aircraft and welcomed new crew, we were instructed as to our role.

Tracker was to head for 'the gap' – the 500-mile stretch in the middle of the North Atlantic run where convoys were out of range of shore-based air protection either from Britain or the Americas. In the course of the disastrous summer of 1942, when U-boats had at first sunk shipping with near-impunity, the Allies had gradually learned how to deal with the danger – and now it was the *Kriegsmarine* that was struggling.

The atmosphere in the convoys was changing; previously, they had seemed like slow-moving funeral corteges processing across a frigid sea, restricted to the speed of the slowest merchantman (sometimes as little as 4 knots) and with ship after ship exploding and breaking apart as they took torpedo hits. Now, there was a growing sense of vengeful exhilaration; the U-boats were being caught and killed.

This was the news and the rumour we heard as we waited in the

Clyde. So far, however, we had flown precisely one day of active convoy protection, on the Murmansk run before *Dasher* had turned back.

In late-summer 1943, *Tracker* sailed from the Clyde for our first escort deployment, instructed to take care of the inward-bound convoy HX258 from Halifax, Nova Scotia (*plate 7*).

Every day, from dawn until dusk and sometimes at night, unless the weather made it impossible we flew the Swordfish off the carrier, patrolling round and round the convoys, flying at an optimum height of around 1,000 feet, at which one was both high enough to see a good stretch of ocean, and low enough to be able to distinguish clearly the white feathering on the water of a submarine periscope. These patrols would last perhaps three hours; the time limits were set by opposing factors. In favour of longer patrols was the danger inherent in deck landings. The longer the patrols, the less often aircraft would have to fly and land again. In favour of shorter patrols was the matter of endurance, a combination of the fuel in our aircraft tanks, and the capacity of our weary minds and our chilled bodies to remain alert in our open cockpits. These were the factors that Freddie Nottingham, as Commander (Flying), would have to assess and balance before he sent us out. We were not all quite as indestructible as he was.

In the air, we must be constantly on high alert: there was, after all, little point in our being up there if we were not watchful enough to see the submarines that would sink the merchantmen and indeed our own carrier beneath us.

Adding to the strain, we must maintain the very strictest radio silence. The U-boats carried a system called Metox (taken from the French) that enabled them to lock onto radio signals and track them. An aircraft making any signal could thus lead a submarine straight to the convoy, in which case rather more than one Swordfish might be lost. Our breaking radio silence in any circumstance other than contact with a U-boat was an offence answerable to a court martial. But if – and only if – we saw a submarine on the surface, or caught a glimpse of a conning tower or periscope, then we would grab at our code books.

I still have my code books from the Western Approaches, and am astonished now at the complexity of the signals that we managed to absorb into our still-young brains. My 'Naval Aircraft Code No. 2' is a numbered copy, with the printed injunction that *Care is to be taken to prevent this book falling into improper hands. In the event of probable capture, it should be sunk in deep water or destroyed.* I sometimes wondered about the circumstances in which the book might be captured separately; in a Swordfish coming down in the sea, we would surely be sunk in deep water together.

As the months went by, my book became littered with amendments carefully annotated in red ink and counter-signed by a second officer. Pasted-in extras reflected the rapid changes of the war. Pages 54–7 gave scores of code signals for all those stirring and magnificent names of the great capital ships of the Royal Navy: HW – 'Howe'; RY – 'Rodney'; TH – 'Temeraire'. But tucked into these pages I find that I have inserted a scrappy little slip of paper, three inches by one inch, printed with a list of ten new names: *Attacker, Battler, Charger, Chaser, Fencer, Pursuer, Stalker, Searcher, Striker, Tracker* – the little escort carriers, like us, thrown together in the last few months and hastily appended. There is no *Dasher*, though, although the ancient *Argus*, our deck landing school, is there in the main listing.

Other slips and changes tell of the increased reliance on our chief weapon in the submarine hunt – our air-surface radar:

Code 414: Have obtained ASV contact – probably a submarine.

Some of the codes were, even then, irredeemably comical. There's a section on 'self-evident code' (a term that teeters towards oxymoron), telling me that ZP was the code for 'zeppelins or blimps'. Another page told me how to report an enemy invasion. I could imagine myself circling high above Britain's beaches desperately flashing *Bishop! Bishop!* to the bemused Home Guard below, who might belatedly recall that this meant, officially: *I have sighted suspicious vessels which I think are probably enemy, but I am not certain.* (How qualified and guarded could you get?)

Some were less amusing. There were, for instance, code signals for identifying British ships that were now at the bottom of the sea, like *Hood* (sunk by the *Bismarck*): that name has a line of red ink through it. There was *Ark Royal*, too, that took the original 816

Squadron down with her; she has a thick, rather smudgy pencil line through her.

This was the language of the intellectual elite of the Navy – us, the observers – communicating our informed judgements directly to our Admiral below. We alone could tell him,

Code 449 / 3

By which I would convey to the Admiral that 'my forecast of enemy movements is that enemy will deploy to starboard.' A string of further numbers and letters would inform the bridge below me exactly which ships the enemy was deploying:

449 – 2 (PT1) A 2 (PT1) E – 3 (PT1) D

which is to say, 'Don't shoot at these – they're British.'

In the 1943 code book, however, submarines are the preoccupation: the signals strike a rising note of urgency.

465 – am over enemy submarine
466 – enemy submarine has dived
470 – have lost touch with enemy submarine…
472/5 – sub on surface and fighting back

After which, the alarm signal – T: torpedo approaching you!

There are footnotes: *If practicable the aircraft is to indicate the exact position of the submarine by a series of dives*. There are also some rapidly pencilled jottings of new codes in my own handwriting, again reflecting changes in the battle:

Code 472 / 9 = possible Schnörkel

Which was to say, this might be one of the modern and much-feared U-boats, the types fitted with breathing apparatus that enabled their diesel motors to operate while submerged. The entry is typical of my meticulousness and my dawning fascination with languages: my hasty jotting is complete with the correct German capital S and umlaut ö.

There were terse codes also for signalling between aircraft:

SA – spread for attack

and:

DV – am in distress.

I had another little booklet issued to me on *Tracker*: the *Western Approaches Convoy Escort Code*. Page two has a form for listing the names of ships present (in pencil to be rubbed out for each new sailing). I can just make out my note of three ships with pretty names – anti-submarine corvettes, I think: *Narcissus* (code name: Rum Punch), *Aconite* (code name: White Lady), and *Lobelia* (code name: Hot Dog).[1] The booklet code words encapsulate desperate situations with fantastical banality, but each with a hint of the vernacular behind them:

Raspberry – ship torpedoed by night. (A spectacular mess.)
Fanny – have attacked without success. (Sweet FA)
Lipstick – must return, short of petrol. (And I need to
powder my nose.)

All these and a hundred others to be memorized by the intellectuals.

So we flew, day after day, round and round. If the weather was fine, we were grateful (*plate 8*). If the sea rose, still we would fly. The 'bats' officer would time our take-off so that the rising bow of the ship would lift the slippery wooden flight deck just as we reached it, tossing us into the air, while on our return my pilot Bobby would attempt to coincide with the stern rising to meet us. That solid patch of stationary concrete at Arbroath was a very distant memory.

*

Then came a change.

In October, we met with a new commander and new tactics. These tactics came from the man who was to become synonymous with U-Boat hunting: Commander Johnnie Walker.[2] Walker already had the ribbons of a DSO and a DSC on his uniform for his prowess in submarine killing. It was Walker who had first thought out a new aggressive approach to defending convoys: instead of the escort forming an anxious screen around the merchantmen, hoping to head off trouble, the hunt would be taken to the submarines: we would go out after them.

As we waited on the Clyde again, our Captain was introduced to

Johnnie Walker's notions (this captain had previously been in charge of a destroyer, and had no experience of commanding a carrier), and we were briefed. We were to join Escort Group 2, Walker's flotilla of sloops of the 'Bird' class, led by HMS *Starling*. The tactics that had evolved meant that the role of carrier-based aircraft was not, principally, to sink the submarines: that fell to Walker's sloops and destroyers, some of which would now be freed from the convoy and able to go out after the U-boats in a semi-independent hunting party. The aircraft prepared the set-up. Constant patrols by rocket-carrying Swordfish forced the submarines to stay submerged; underwater, their speed was so reduced that they could not keep up with the convoys. It would be more and more difficult for them to transmit information about the convoy to other members of the wolf pack as it tried to gather for an attack. Underwater, the submarines were vulnerable to detection by the ASDIC[3] on the destroyers. If the more daring U-boat commanders came to the surface, the aircraft would spot them and direct the sloops with depth charges towards them. While the sloops were closing in, the Swordfish could attack firing rockets with solid war-heads, which were tricky to aim but could be highly effective; they were intended to plunge into the water just short of a U-boat and rise up to punch holes in the underside of the pressure hull, and on occasion Swordfish rockets drilled right through the hull of a U-boat and emerged in the water on the other side.

Attached to Walker's Escort Group 2, we took convoy ONB207 outwards, sailing west towards Newfoundland on 2 October 1943.

We had a journalist with us on *Tracker*, a war correspondent. His name was A.D. Divine,[4] and, inevitably, he was known as Father Divine. He wrote for the *Daily Sketch* in London, and was working on an 'Atlantic diary' to hearten British readers. He seemed to have unfettered access to every part of the carrier, popping up on the bridge one moment, in the hangar the next.

Father Divine's accounts of the convoy were published in the *Daily Sketch* over three days in January 1944.[5] They made for a stirring read:

> We have gone on the offensive in the Atlantic. The days
> when we maintained only a thin and desperate watch upon

our most important convoys have long since passed ... As I write, we are making contact with a convoy strung over the whole arc of the horizon to the north-west. We are going to cover it through the area of a particularly heavy concentration of U-boats ... Officially we are called a Support Group – actually we are a hunting pack, a super-pack to break the wolf-pack methods of the U-boat ...

When we reached U-boats and the hunt began, Father Divine got into his stride:

An hour ago, a U-boat died. We did not kill it. It was ahead of us, out of sight of the convoy with which we still move, a lone U-boat lying in the gap. But another group was operating far ahead. We heard the story of the submarine's destruction coming over the air in the terse staccato of the wireless signals.

First of all came to us, listening in the control room in our carrier, the brief notation of the bearing and distance of the 'echo'. Thereafter the thing became almost cold, almost blood-curdling in its passionless efficiency. Ship after ship of the group ahead made contact. We heard cross-bearings; we heard the course of the U-boat, the speed as it tried to crawl away secretly and silently in the depth of the Atlantic ...

At 10.50 a.m. we heard the first attack go in. The minutes went by; other attacks were made. By half-past eleven it was clear that the U-boat was already crippled. At 11.47 the senior officer of our group [Johnnie Walker] sent a signal: 'Rally and smite him, for the Lord hath delivered him into thy hand.' Again we heard the attacks go in. After a little while came the reply: 'Smitten thrice like Jonah he remains deep and I doubt he will rise again.'

We heard another attack. Then, abruptly, ribaldry came over the empty air from many miles ahead of us: 'Hearse summoned.'

*

There were curiously peaceful interludes, even on these convoys, even knowing that we could never be sure where the U-boats were, or whether the carrier might be torpedoed as we slept. Sometimes, sailing for long spells in circles above the ships, I could become quite dreamy. I wrote more poems, putting myself in the third-person:

> Once, far out on the Western Ocean,
> Flying back to his ship at sunset
> He had seen twenty miles south
> A flutter of white wings on the water.
> He altered course to investigate –
> Great sails ballooned and sagged:
> Sixteen Portuguese fishing barques
> Curtseying in convoy for the Azores …

But such times were not common. As before, our worst adversary was often the Atlantic weather. In one gale, in November 1943, *Tracker* was almost lost.

That morning the ship's Meteorological Officer had sent up a balloon to take a measurement of wind speed. As the ship rolled, part of his equipment skipped over the side of the rolling ship into the sea. The company joked that, in losing this, he lost control of the storm.

By mid-afternoon the wind was freshening rapidly. *Tracker*, like all the escort carriers, was terrible in a heavy sea; she rolled and pitched far worse than the low-slung cruisers or the heavily weighted merchantmen with their holds full of tanks and wheat. For the crew, this meant a relentless attrition of fatigue and injury: men slipped and fell heavily against ladders, bulkheads and piping; arms were broken, heads cut open. One could scarcely sleep, since merely lying in a bunk required clinging onto the sides to prevent oneself being tipped onto the cabin floor. Besides which, almost every fitting on *Tracker* was steel, and banged, clanged and groaned without cease. Father Divine remarked that it was like trying to sleep in a boiler factory.

By that evening it was howling a full gale, with a high sea pouring icily down upon us. At 22.00 hours *Tracker* was ordered to alter course, a direction that would leave her beam-on to the running sea. (For all his skill and brilliance, we sometimes resented Commander

Johnnie Walker who would get excited at the sniff of a U-boat and go haring off in his agile, purpose-built submarine-hunting sloop, *Starling*. We wondered whether he had the least idea of how ungainly an aircraft carrier was; we rather wished someone would tell him before he gave these orders.) A signal was piped through the ship: 'Stand by for heavy rolling'. The ship began to wallow to an extent no one on board had ever experienced before. Those on the bridge went very white as they watched the roll-and-pitch indicator. To their disbelief, the ship heeled over an astonishing 52 degrees – a Navy record – more or less lying on her side and surely bound to capsize … but after an eternity, she shuddered her way upright, only to do it all again a moment later. The lumbering *Tracker*, with her flight deck high above the superstructure, seemed certain to flip over, but in fact the wooden decking was relatively light and the ship's centre of gravity was lower than it looked.

I was on deck, helping to secure equipment. As the ship went into another astonishing roll I was flung off my feet and began sliding helplessly towards the side of the flight deck; if I was lucky I would end up in the catwalk or, if unlucky, in the sea. I grabbed at one of the arrestor wires, which saved me, but the wire had been thickly greased and, although I did not go over the edge, I now slithered absurdly up and down the wire before I could find a purchase and grope my way inside.

Down in the hangar, all was chaos; at 52 degrees the floor was more of a wall than a floor. The Swordfish created their own problems. More modern aircraft (such as Seafires) folded their wings upwards, but there was never anything modern about a Swordfish: its wings would be unclipped and swung on large hinges back alongside the fuselage, the wingtips fixed to the tailplane by a short steel rod. The constant rolling of the ship would weaken the rod and its fastenings, and this would be made worse if the wings were heavy with bomb racks or rocket launchers. We did not like to take the launchers off, as this could affect their alignment and accuracy, but in heavy weather there was no choice: the launchers were lowered to the floor of the hangar and held down with straps.

But now everything had broken free. Our aircraft had thrown off their securing cables and were slithering about inside the echoing interior like maddened, terrified animals, wrecking anything in their path, and with riggers clinging to every part of them. There were sheets of spilled oil that took men's feet out from under them, so that fitters, aircrew and sailors went tumbling through the hangar, taking injury after injury. There were broken batteries spilling pools of acid that reeked and burned one's nose. There were loose tools flying through the hangar space, threatening our faces. Freddie Nottingham was there in the midst of the squadron, roaring commands and grabbing at Swordfish that seemed determined to destroy themselves, the ship, and the crew, with their wings loose and swinging freely in a cacophony of snapping wires and struts, while the men swarmed about with ropes and cables, lashing them to anything solidly fixed, or trying to lasso heavy equipment as it slithered past on the spilled oil. At one point a furious spray of liquid began which, to anyone in 816 Squadron, could only suggest one thing: aviation fuel – exactly that which had probably blown *Dasher* apart. But after an agonizing moment the spray turned to a solid jet, and we realized that the spray was water, extremely cold water: a fire hydrant had been smashed and was busily pumping the Atlantic at us (as though we weren't uncomfortable enough already). Only when *Tracker*'s course altered again and we were head into the seas could any semblance of normality return.

When dawn came, we found that we had just two Swordfish fit to fly.

Not that there could be any flying in such conditions. It was intensely frustrating, and more than that: it was frightening, because if we were not flying we were not seeing the submarines that wanted to sink us. One could never sleep securely for fear of torpedoes (some people rested with their cabin doors wedged open, lest they became damaged and distorted, trapping you inside). The squadron fitters worked in sixteen-hour shifts to reconstruct our aircraft, cannibalizing those that were smashed beyond hope to assemble something that could be flown: a wing section from one, undercarriage from another... But until the gale and the sea subsided, there was nothing we could do but let Johnnie Walker hunt submarines by means of ASDIC, 'huff-duff' radio location, binoculars and his unnervingly accurate instinct. As we cowered in the sheltered depths of *Tracker*, we could hear depth charges exploding.

One evening, yet another gale began: the bridge anemometer was rising steadily, the bow of the ship rising and falling through seventy feet. In such conditions, not only could we not fly but, with the crashing seas, the escort destroyers were thrown this way and that and could make little use even of their ASDIC, so that a U-boat might well be able to catch us unawares.

But by late 1943 the mood in the Atlantic had changed dramatically. Eighteen months previously, the more cavalier U-boat captains had run riot in the convoys; by now, so many of them had been killed – and so efficient had the combination of air, radar and ASDIC become – that they were fearful and shy of contact. Now, U-boats might circle quite close to a convoy without attacking.

This evening, however, the convoy and a U-boat came upon each other by surprise. Throughout *Tracker*, alarm bells began to ring, sending men running. The U-boat had been spotted on the surface passing down one side of the convoy; the submarine's commander was taking the chance of what had seemed like a lull in the battle to re-charge her batteries. The U-boat hastily swung towards the convoy and fired two torpedoes at us in the gloom: one missed completely, and a moment later we heard a dull thud, as the second exploded harmlessly in open water. At once, two of the convoy escorts turned about to search for the U-boat, but in the gale and the high seas and gloom, could not find it. Now the gale rose still further, reaching a force 11 severe storm; *Tracker* had no choice but to turn into the wind and remain stationary to avoid foundering. So we lingered all the rest of that night, with the knowledge that somewhere in the water near us there was a submarine.

There were two pieces of German technology for which we were immensely grateful: their magnetic triggers, which were very unreliable and often went off in the wrong place; and their GNAT acoustic torpedoes (which were supposed to home in on the high-speed screws of a warship), which were so crude that they could often be fooled by a couple of steel pipes allowed to clang together, trailed on a cable behind the ship.

Not long afterwards, in another storm, I went to sit out an hour or two in the control room of the HF/DF ('huff-duff'), the high-frequency radio locator system that could pinpoint the presence of an enemy transmitter. The controllers had identified a U-boat following us on the surface at a position some twelve miles astern of *Tracker*. After an interminable and frustrating wait, the officer in charge of the huff-duff turned to me: 'Isn't there any way you fellows can have a go at him?'

We both knew very well the problems in ranging a Swordfish in such conditions, but I felt I had to ask. I went looking for Freddie Nottingham.

'Freddie, there's this Hun just sitting on the surface twelve miles astern of us and laughing at us and signalling our position. They're watching him in the huff-duff plot. They want to know if we couldn't possibly get at him – couldn't we? I'll come with you.'

This last was pure bravado.

'Here's a keen lad,' smiled Freddie. 'I'll go and talk to the Captain. You'd better go and ask Brian if he thinks it might be possible to range a serviceable aircraft.'

Thank God, the whole venture was turned down. We would have put ourselves and the whole escort group at unacceptable risk.

*

We were winning. We felt that we were winning, even if most of the time we were either cold or petrified or both. Now both the Swordfish and the escort ships had radar systems that in a reasonable sea could pick out a conning tower at a good distance; surfacing by night was no long safe for the U-boats. One morning very early, just after 2 a.m., there was a kerfuffle, and we hurried out onto the deck to see if a merchantman had been hit. But no: a submarine had been detected on the surface by radar on the destroyer HMS *Kite*, and now the night sky turned fiery white with star shells. Moments later, in the dying light we heard the crashing of depth charges as the escort sloops and corvettes pounced. In *Tracker*'s control rooms we listened to the radio exchanges of instructions and coordinates as Walker closed in, the U-boat attempting to flee underwater but now with the ASDIC of half a dozen hunters locked onto her. At dawn, *Tracker's* Swordfish flew off, searching. At breakfast, the ship's loudspeakers relayed the news sent back from the air, of the wreckage sighted: a smashed torpedo; woodwork from the submarine's fittings; items of clothing and bedding, and then corpses floating.

That same afternoon, *U842* was sighted by another of *Tracker's* Swordfish; the aircraft circled over the spot as the submarine dived in desperation. Though soon there was no visible sign of her, still the Swordfish circled as the sloops rushed closer, for the U-boat underwater could move at barely 4 knots on her electric motors. For some two hours they tracked and plotted her movements, releasing patterns of depth charges; at 3.25 p.m. the kill was reported, the wreckage and oil there on the surface.

Two kills in one day, and one hundred young men dead under the sea.

*

The arrival of the escort carriers had, it was now loudly proclaimed, reversed the odds in the Battle of the Atlantic. We were finding fewer and fewer U-boats; the Germans were taking such a battering that they were hard-pressed to get wolf packs together at all. On these convoy escorts, we maintained our patrols and searches, flying all day every day as long as the weather allowed, although at a cost of several aircraft.

For the strain told on 816 Squadron; for our younger aircrew in particular, the experience must have been stupefyingly frightening and exhausting; in the poor weather we seemed to be perpetually wet and cold, and we seldom rested properly. First patrols flew off before dawn. They would return in time for a fresh patrol to set out before midday, another mid-afternoon and another before dusk.

I cannot say whether it was harder for pilots or observers; we worked together. The FAA was often criticized – with regard to its commissioning new aircraft designs – for having insisted on a crew of at least two: a pilot and an observer-navigator. This meant that aircraft were heavier and slower, so that (for instance) the otherwise rather good Fairey Firefly, intended as a fighter, was considerably slower than enemy single-seaters. But then, those enemy fighters and those design critics never flew over the North Atlantic or above Arctic convoys; they never experienced the terrible strain of knowing that – although one was constantly tired and sleep-deprived – one's survival depended on accurate dead reckoning to bring one back to a tiny flight deck bobbing about in the sea. The FAA demanded a crew of two because it was surely all too much for one man.

I know I owed my life to my pilot Bobby Creighton many times over. The strain on observers was rather different, a constant wearying concentration that wore me down. From the moment we took to the air, I was watching the surface below for tell-tale signs of U-boats. I was also scanning the cathode ray tube of our ASV radar, which could pick out a periscope in a decent sea and give me a bearing on the screen. At the same time, I was plotting and calculating by the charts on the wooden board on my knees, estimating windspeed by the white spume off the waves or, if conditions allowed, by that primitive business of dropping smokefloats in the sea (see p.41). I seemed to be looking in all directions at once, and doing sums about them all – and if I got any of these calculations wrong, it was more than likely that we would be lost.

It was very easy to make errors. I knew I could do all the calculations; I knew that I was more than proficient at that. But with the weariness, the sleeplessness, the fear, the cold…

Bobby said, 'I owe you my life, too.' And George, our air gunner, agreed. Sometimes they hardly liked to speculate what would happen if I got my sums wrong. They kept me well supplied with coffee and chocolate to keep me alert and thinking clearly.

The calculations that saved us were a joint effort: Bobby's estimates of our remaining fuel and flying time, and my reckoning of our course. If we were patrolling astern of the convoy, there was a particularly agonizing fear of being left behind. The old Swordfish, with its wires, wheels and double wings dragging the air, and its primitive fixed-pitch propeller, simply could not hurry after its mother ship. We flew at 80 or 85 knots. If a headwind of 40 knots got up, we would be chasing *Tracker* at just forty knots. But add to that *Tracker* steaming away from us at perhaps ten or fifteen knots, and our fuel tanks emptying...

We had a squadron song that we would sing drunkenly to Judy Garland's tune, to drown those fears:

> Somewhere over the ocean,
>   Far from gay –
> Somewhere over the ocean,
>   Far from our ETA.
> Somehow I vaguely wonder
>   With remorse
> If I made a slight blunder
>   In working out the course.
>
> We try the wireless: not a sound.
> They'll never know where we were drowned.
> They won't much mind.
> The beacon's mile's off tune. I think
> We're going to end up in the drink
> And there they'll find us...
>
> Drifting over the ocean
>   Miles away,
> Drifting over the ocean
>   After our ETA.

But many afternoons I stood for real at the back of the flight deck, looking astern for a Swordfish that had not yet caught up with us, wondering where my friends were.

And of course, catching up with us was only half the problem. The aircraft still had to land.

Each patrol had to find that 'gyrating cricket pitch' which might well have moved position unexpectedly, if Johnnie Walker's extraordinary nose for U-boats had led him to order *Tracker* to a new position – in which case, given the strictly-enforced radio silence, the aircrew would have to frantically scan the sea below to find her. Every landing-on was perilous, and to this day I suffer from back pain as a result of crumbled vertebrae, the consequence of repeated crash-landings on aircraft carriers.

I can recall – frequently – watching a Swordfish approach for a seemingly faultless landing, only to have the stern of the ship rise too fast on the swell, to meet the aircraft too abruptly, snapping the undercarriage and sending the Swordfish skidding and tumbling, crumpling wings and spars or perhaps breaking the fuselage in half, while other aircraft of the patrol circled patiently, watching, waiting their turn. Then another would drop down and smash into the barriers. The flight-deck riggers would pounce on her, heaving the wreck aside to make way for a third aircraft's attempt (*plate 9*).

Bobby Creighton once achieved the spectacular feat of writing off three aircraft in one go. Our hook missed all the arrestor wires and the batsman had waved us off and round again – always an alarming procedure, with the aircraft frantically scrabbling for power and airspeed to get clear of the deck and the sea. Bobby opened up to full throttle and pulled the stick to go back up; the Swordfish had responded and we had started to climb steeply – but at this moment the trailing hook caught the top wire of the barrier protecting parked aircraft. Just in front of this barrier, a group of fitters and riggers were folding the wings of the previously landed planes. I looked straight down from my cockpit into the terrified face of one of the riggers as the Swordfish stopped dead in the air and came down on top of them. The rigger let go of the wing he was holding and it swung with a smash into the side of its fuselage, which sent that aircraft crashing into another. The rigger was thrown out of harm's way, but it was a shambles. I don't remember anybody being seriously hurt on this occasion, but the look on that man's face has haunted me ever since.

Sometimes an aircraft would miss not only the arrestor wires but indeed most of the flight deck. In my *Manual of Seamanship* there are instructions on retrieving an aircraft from the sea; these instructions have a curious air to them that is slightly unreal and not quite calm, and that hints at the difficulties involved:

> It is very important to have plenty of steadying lines on the machine. An aircraft tends to turn head to wind when suspended, and therefore if possible she should be turned head to wind first. If not possible, she should be lifted two or three feet and then slewed slowly round... At the earliest opportunity, steadying lines should be attached to the wing

tips. The crew of the aircraft will climb out on the planes [wings] for this purpose… Spars should be manned to control the aircraft and prevent the planes fouling the ship's side. The most satisfactory ones are bamboo poles fitted with a padded T-piece at one end, but emergency ones can be improvised with soft broom heads lashed to boathook staves.

The crew will sit out on the wings. Sailors will push it away with a broom…

And that is not an emergency, but a 'routine' retrieval of a floatplane (some Swordfish were fitted with floats). Two pages later comes another chapter: 'Salving a Wrecked Aircraft':

All fleet air arm aircraft are made as buoyant as possible and arrangements are made to jettison the petrol and so use the tank as an aid to buoyancy. The pilot, however, may not have time to achieve the latter. When an aircraft is floating in the water, the engine will probably take the nose down and the tail only may be above the surface. [If you can haul it up on a derrick,] slash everywhere with a knife or boat hook to let the water out.

Notice the lower case 'fleet air arm'. Two other priorities are established here:

In all cases it is important to remember that the engine is the most important part of the machine to salve… Dismantled portions of damaged aircraft are not to be thrown over the side without first removing or obliterating the national marking…

Keep the engine, and leave no trace. Could one imagine any of this in the Atlantic or the Arctic? Did they remove the national markings before pushing the wrecked Sea Hurricanes off *Dasher*? Or when one of *Tracker*'s Swordfish had missed the wires and gone over the side? I watched friends bringing their Swordfish ever so gently down onto *Tracker* – only to see them tossed into the sea, the consequence not of enemy action but of a tiny misjudgement or sheer bloody luck.

I was idling up on the bridge one day: a sequence of photographs records the disaster I now witnessed (*plates 10–13*). I watched a Swordfish nearing the flight deck in a model approach – but then everything went appallingly wrong. The aircraft must have caught a wingtip on something as the ship rolled. Or perhaps a tyre burst. For whatever reason, she slewed violently to the right, skidding towards the deck hands who cowered in the catwalks – and flopped straight over the starboard side.

The Swordfish was in the water right alongside the ship, just below me in the bridge; in the first photograph, one can see that she is still well afloat although in a seethe of white foam. The three aircrew are clambering out. In the next photo, taken only moments later, you can see that she is beginning to sink – the top wing is now down on the water – and that she is drifting astern, for although *Tracker*'s screws have stopped, the ship does not, of course, come to an instant halt. In this second picture you can see also the damage that the aircraft has caused to the ship's radio masts: on an escort carrier, these projected out sideways to be clear of the flight deck. And you can see the aircrew's friends crowding into a gun emplacement to yell encouragement. In the third photo, the Swordfish is now well down by the nose, her hefty Pegasus dragging her under – and the aircrew are not yet safe! Meanwhile, far astern of the carrier, a second Swordfish can be glimpsed as little more than a speck, heading for the carrier, but unable to land because the flight deck is crowded with running, shouting men.

In the last photo, the aircraft is almost gone. Only her tail remains, jutting forlornly from the sea, a last pocket of air in the rear fuselage holding her briefly up. The second Swordfish passes over, looking out for survivors.

The air gunner was saved, as was the pilot, Lefty Bissett. But Jack Stretton, the observer, was drowned and lost.

We could not stop and search, but had to keep up with the convoy we were there to protect, and to keep moving lest we provide a sitting target for a torpedo. It is difficult to describe the anguish of looking out from the stern of the ship, knowing that your colleague and friend is somewhere there in the water, and knowing that there is nothing you can do or say, and that you are steaming steadily away from him.

Notes

1. Three 'Flower' class corvettes.
2. John Walker had been on the verge of retirement at the outbreak of the Second World War, his Navy career having been not particularly distinguished. In convoy protection, however, he found his metier, and he became the most successful submarine hunter of the war. But on his return from these convoys in November, it was to the news that his own son Timothy had been killed serving in a British submarine in the Mediterranean.
3. The British Second World War name for what is now called sonar.
4. Arthur Durham Divine (1904–87), also known as David Divine. He was a prolific writer who also published accounts of Dunkirk and other naval operations.
5. *Daily Sketch*, 3, 4 and 8 January 1944.

CHAPTER SIX

Newfoundland

Led by the famous slayer of submarines, Captain Johnnie Walker, we sailed through thick fog into Argentia, Newfoundland.[1] What an extraordinary place. Argentia had been built by the Americans at the time of the original Lend-Lease agreement; Winston Churchill had come here in August 1941, sailing in HMS *Prince of Wales* to thrash out the original deal with President Roosevelt.[2] The base was well protected with magnetic anti-submarine booms and spotter blimps[3] (*plate 14*), and it was vast, supposedly large enough to accommodate the entire Royal Navy in the event of the British capitulating to the Nazis. This gave me a slightly odd feeling on arrival, as though perhaps I had misunderstood the situation and we had surrendered after all, and were fleeing in ignominy.

But as *Tracker* and Escort Group Two approached, word got round Argentia that the celebrated Captain Walker was coming, that he had destroyed three U-boats for the loss of not one ship of the convoy. There was a military band waiting on the quay, and as the 'baby flat-top' *Tracker* came alongside they struck up a triumphal march – only to realize that Johnnie Walker was actually in the destroyer just behind us. The band stopped dead in the middle of their tune, recommencing exactly where they had left off when the hero's own ship approached.

Here we saw the American scale of things. I was proudly informed that 5,000 tons of topsoil had been brought from Missouri to make a lawn for the Commander-in-Chief's garden, with thousands of tons more for the construction of tennis courts. The US Army and the Air Force were there also, and each service had its own barracks and cinemas, mess halls and bars and wardrooms, supplied with foods and luxuries that we of the Royal Navy and FAA hardly dreamed of. Brian Bennett muttered that, by comparison, at Scapa Flow there was nothing but the Officer's Club on Flotta where one might, if one was lucky, find a boiled egg to eat and a few sheep to chase by way of entertainment.

Here they entertained us nobly – so nobly that, the night we sailed from Argentia, I dreamed that I was sailing in a beautiful glass ship full of brown ale. But any dreams we might have had of extended rest were cut short. Argentia was not a holiday: we were to collect fuel and replacement aircraft that had been thoughtfully placed there in waiting for us. The 816 Squadron troops had achieved remarkable feats of cannibalization, sticking together bits of hurricane-wrecked Swordfish and Seafires in the most imaginative ways, such that they were proudly able to give us five of each aircraft to fly onshore for full maintenance. The squadron, however, was battered and bruised, and we needed thorough servicing. With true American bustle, repairs were effected in just a few days, and we set to sea again.

But *Tracker*, too, had been injured; as she had lurched at extraordinary angles in one of the gales, one of her main generators had been seriously damaged and it was beyond the facilities of Argentia to fix. We were directed to Norfolk, Virginia. Even before we reached there, a team of American engineers came aboard and set about cutting a large hole in the steel decking of the hangar; as soon as we docked in Norfolk, the entire generator was lifted out through this hole and swung ashore for mending.

This gave us a week – and at last we were told we could have time ashore. And as I looked out at the lush landscape and thriving main streets of Virginia, one thought above all others came to mind: birdseed.

It was a distant memory, but it came crowding back. I recalled *Dasher*, and bobbing about in that Icelandic fjord as the storms subsided briefly and the convoy gathered for Murmansk. As *Dasher* had set off through the rising sea, there had been no question of anyone flying, and so there had been little for the 816 Squadron aircrew to do but read. We never had enough to read; Don Ridgway remembered from an earlier ship devouring all the works of Dickens, the life of the Buddha and some well-thumbed copies of *Men Only*. On *Dasher* we had borrowed each other's books, but soon ran out of those. We'd read quite enough of the *Manual of*

Seamanship. Desperately, we had searched the ship for literature – and someone had found a copy of *Cage Birds Monthly.* Never mind what it was doing on an aircraft carrier: Ken Horsfield, Brian and I had all read it from cover to cover, while standing jammed between steam piping for warmth. I had read about the smartest new cages, the sweetest-voiced canaries and the prettiest of prize-winning budgies; I'd read reports from competitions, and debates on issues of breeding and incubation. When I had read all that, I turned to the back pages and read the small ads. And there, I had noticed a heart-felt plea from a gentleman in Beckenham: he was offering a fortune – £100 per hundredweight – for budgerigar seed.

For the budgies of Britain were starving. In the darkest hours of the Battle of the Atlantic, the Lend-Lease agreement and the convoy planners had made no provision for bringing urgently needed birdseed past the U-boat Wolf Packs. Perhaps they might have stuffed every Sherman tank with canary food, but by some awful oversight this had not been done. The gentleman in Beckenham was in a fearful state, and his prize-winning stock of breeding budgies were nearing the end…

£100 per hundredweight: I remembered this as *Tracker* came into the quayside at Norfolk, and had her generator winched out. Virginia, surely, was birdseed country.

I would need transport. I told a flagrant lie, persuading someone that I was *Tracker's* catering officer, and I was allocated a jeep with a volunteer driver called Katy. She drove me down to the ferry across Chesapeake Bay. As we waited at one set of traffic lights she glowered at a large truck drawing up in the lane alongside us. The driver of the truck was a black man. Katy leaned across me and bawled: 'Git out of my way, yu goddam black Satan!'

She saw my astonishment, and said: 'Yaw south of the Mason-Dixon line here, Limey.'

She left me to walk onto the ferry, where I was taught another lesson in American history. I was walking around on the upper deck when a man approached me with a little tray from which he was peddling shoelaces and boxes of matches. I took a pair of laces and reached into my pocket to pay, placing a coin on his tray. He regarded it suspiciously: 'What's that? Hey, that's Limey dough!'

I hastily picked it up again, digging quickly for something else.

'I'm terribly sorry…'

'That's OK, son – but how come you carry Limey dough?'

'Well, I'm a Limey.'

He put his tray down on a capstan and studied me with interest.

'Is that so? A Limey. Hey, you gotta king over there, ain't yer?'

'Yes, that's right.'

'Son, you get rid of him. We had a king here once, in the old days. We got rid of him. Been much better since.'

When the ferry docked, I went walking up the main street – and almost the first shop I came to was a corn-chandler's. I went in.

'Do you sell birdseed? For budgerigars?'

'Sure do.'

'Could you keep me three hundredweight? I'll pay you for it now, and come back for it at the end of the week.'

'Three hundredweight? Sure can!'

I paid him some modest sum, sixpence a pound I think.

For a week, we killed time, many of the crew learning to drink rum and Coca-Cola in the best Andrews Sisters manner (i.e. in the company of young ladies of the town). On Saturday, once more posing as *Tracker*'s caterer, I talked my way into another US Navy jeep and driver, and went back to collect my seed, taking with me three green kitbags in which to put it. The shop man greeted me cheerfully: trade was looking up.

'Say, it's a good job you asked me to keep that seed for you. Only half an hour after, another Limey came in and bought my whole stock.'

I quickly thought back to *Dasher*, and at once had an image of Brian Bennett and Ken Horsfield amongst the steam piping engrossed in *Cage Birds Monthly*.

'What did he look like? Did he have a long straggly beard and a moustache?'

'Sure did – that's the guy! You know him?'

That was Ken.

With my kitbags filled and in the jeep, I returned to the ship, persuading one of the stewards to help me carry them rather quickly on board before anyone asked questions. In my cabin, I stuffed them into the wardrobe; there was little room for anything else. Then I went looking for Ken. He was lying stretched out on his bunk, with a pleased look of dreamy calculation.

'All right, Ken – where have you stowed it? We went to the same merchant.'

I flung open his cupboard: it was packed from floor to ceiling with large cardboard boxes from which there trickled just a trace of budgie seed.

He was in a joint venture with Brian, his pilot.

*

We sailed out of Norfolk on 5 December 1943, joining our next Atlantic convoy, HX270, out of Halifax (Nova Scotia) bound for Liverpool. Every day we kept up that same monotonous cycle of patrolling from dawn to dusk, round and round above the convoy, straining our eyes at the sea below.

A Swordfish pilot on *Tracker*, John Moore, wrote a little booklet about her – *Escort Carrier* – published during the war and printed on rough war-standard paper, and describing those Atlantic convoys. It is a piece of propaganda, designed to fill the reader with confidence in our modern sea-air power and our eagerness for the chase; it says nothing of the fear, exhaustion and depression that often filled us. Moore's booklet is all of forty-eight pages, but it has plentiful evocative photographs, and many of us acquired a copy as a souvenir. Moore wasn't allowed to name the ship, but to anyone who sailed in her it is obviously *Tracker*, and when I look at my copy now I remember how limited life was in certain respects, and how novel in others.

When not flying, there was very little to do; we would read or play cards or write letters, or just wander through the ship. Moore's photographs show the Swordfish aircrew hanging about in the catwalks alongside the flight decks gossiping with the emergency crews, sharing cigarettes and getting in their way; I remember that. Next we'd drift into the hangar that always smelled of the dope used on the Swordfish wings, and where the torpedoes, painted a glossy blue, were strapped into racks about the sides together with fire-extinguishers, tools and more tools, and the ladders that allowed the mechanics to swarm all over the Swordfish. Even in a calm sea, everything was lashed tight, ladders, buckets and tool boxes, lest some slight lurch might send a heavy object buffeting a hole in an aircraft's fabric flanks. The fitters would be reassembling engines or cannibalizing two broken Swordfish into one functional one – and we'd get in the way there also. No smoking down here, of course – whenever possible, aircraft were refuelled out on deck – but after the explosion on *Dasher* we didn't need to be reminded about fuel and smoking.

We'd go and visit friends in the sick bay, marvelling at the medical provision American ships made: Moore shows us *Tracker*'s operating theatre, which had three emergency lighting systems, several sterilizing autoclaves and the instruments to fill them, multifunctional operating tables that could be swivelled and raised by foot pedals – the sort of thing any dentist has today, but they certainly weren't seen in the average British warship in 1943. There were drawers stuffed with gloves and syringes, and a complete pathology lab with microscopes and incubators for bacteria (not that, in 1943, we had much in the way of antibiotics to treat them, probably only sulphonamides). There was even an x-ray machine.

We would eat much better on the homeward run than the outward, for the catering officers (the real ones) would provision the ship with everything that in Britain was rationed but in America was freely available. *Tracker* had other features that in 1943 were a great novelty, at least to British crews. Food was no longer fetched, as in Navy tradition, by a man detailed from each mess to go and get it, so that it was usually lukewarm by the time it reached you and you'd likely miss your meal anyway if you were on watch. No: on *Tracker* meals were served, always hot, in a 'cafeteria', a notion to which new crew had to be introduced. This was such a marvel that it merits a photo in Moore's booklet, with dazed and happy crewmen beaming down at the food they've just collected from the serving hatch. There were special steel trays with recessed compartments – one for the meat, one for the vegetables, one for the pudding – so that each man only brought his cutlery, while the size of the tray recesses determined the serving portions.

The galleys had any number of marvels, things that would seem entirely mundane now but which in the 1940s were evidence of the American gift for gadgetry and 'labor-saving', and that only caught on in Britain after the war. Everything was electric. Instead of teams of ratings spud-bashing, there were electric potato-peeling machines that tumbled the potatoes over and over in a drum lined with coarse metal flecks. The mixers, the slicers, the ovens – everything was electric. *Tracker's* bakery produced 500lb of white bread a day, and it was real bread, what's more: the appalling 'Chorleywood' process of steam-baked sliced pap that ruined British baking had not yet been invented. *Tracker* carried twenty tons of flour, not the gritty grey-brown stuff that my wife Gina was putting up with in London (and which kept poorly at sea), but finest Canadian white, gluten-strong, the very best for bread-making.

It being an American-built ship, there was no provision for a daily rum ration, for the US Navy sailed dry. But *Tracker* had another novelty: soda fountains, with flavouring concentrates: strawberry, raspberry, orange, lemon-and-lime… They could even make ice-cream. Convoys leaving the US and sailing for Britain would stock up on delights such as Coca-Cola, although the supplies never lasted the voyage.

So we ate and drank rather well, sailing west-to-east.

We'd sleep or relax as best we could, more or less fully dressed so as to be able to scramble to our action stations if the alarms went. We were two or four officers to a cabin in narrow wooden bunks, with fans for the heat (in the North Atlantic…) and with a folding desk containing a little communal safe, our personal binoculars and endless packs of cigarettes (we all smoked heavily). Moore has a photo of a cabin; there are centrefolds from *Men Only* taped to the steel walls. Our cabins were filled with photographs of women, some of them our wives and girlfriends, some of them rather obviously not. Officers' cabins were on the second deck just beneath the hangar; this was not ideal, being well to the stern and thus very susceptible to the pitching of the ship. American-built ships didn't have hammocks even for the ratings; everyone got a bunk, so all those early pages of instruction in my *Manual of Seamanship*, about how to 'rove the hammock's lanyard and trice it up', were quite redundant. Bunks were modern, were comfortable – except that they had insufficient restraints to stop us tumbling: in the sorts of storms we encountered, you'd be tipped out on your head instead of swinging gracefully in your hammock. If the seas were really bad, some of us put our mattresses on the floor where we'd likely all end up in a heap.

There were other rooms and compartments in *Tracker* that, thanks to John Moore and his photographs, I now remember. There was (he describes) the ASDIC chamber with the 'grave intent watchkeepers'. There was the post office, 'fitted up so like a village post office that it gives one a sharp nostalgia for home'. There was a laundry – a laundry! Even battleships often did without a laundry. The Americans, however, had assumed that a civilized warship needed a laundry, and had created space to give us one. The Royal Navy was not going to pay for such pampering (we were only at sea for a few weeks at a time, what need clean clothes…) but faced with an allocation of space, they had not objected to a bank loan being obtained with which to buy American laundry equipment. We had to pay for laundering our clothes, but that money paid off the loan for the purchase.

Most marvellous of all for Moore was the gyro room, deep down in the forward part of the ship, filled with the high-pitched whispering hum of the Sperry gyro-compass, the master of all the ship's gyros, spinning like a top in its case, 'one of the loveliest and most complicated pieces of machinery every devised'. The Electrical Artificer who attends it, says Moore, 'serves it as a priest serves his idol'.

There is also in the book a photo of the parachute packing room, which Moore in his upbeat way describes as possessing a queer beauty, with its long polished packing table, 'hung around with dozens of parachutes of pale daffodil yellow, and dinghies of bright chrome'. As he says, the FAA never used white parachutes, because the foam on the sea was white and a yellow chute was more likely to be seen. Moore mentions that we aircrew would covet all that silk, thinking of giving it to our wives and girlfriends for making pyjamas. What he does not say is that, at sea, pyjamas were about all a parachute was good for. The thought of dropping into the sea was quite appalling: our chances of survival were so minimal. The ship's surgeon gave lectures on surviving in an open boat, but no one was fooled. We all knew the survival rates: when *Ark Royal* had been sunk, more than 500 men had died. When *Bismarck* had been caught and destroyed, of her company of nearly 2,000 only 110 had survived. And these ships had both been lost well to the south of the usual convoy routes. Nearer the Arctic ice, the water was so cold that (it was said) the blood would freeze in the veins in six minutes – or was it three minutes? The chances of an escort corvette finding us and pulling us from the water in time were hardly worth calculating.

John Moore witnessed another aircraft crashing off *Tracker* into the sea, and described in those same terms of horror watching what might become of our friends. One evening, the aircrew pottering about in the catwalks saw a patrolling Swordfish return. Conditions were fair enough: passable visibility, rough seas but not too much of a swell. But that little could be enough for a catastrophe. The first of the Swordfish came in astern in a model approach run, only to have *Tracker's* stern lift suddenly, smacking the undercarriage of the Swordfish, which now bounced forward just as the bow of the ship had dropped, the flight deck falling away beneath the aircraft. The Swordfish stalled and slewed – and dropped over the side, its three-and-a-half tons smacking into the water and breaking up; almost immediately the nose went down with the weight of the Pegasus engine, the tail of the aircraft lifting into the air like a white whale's fluke. The crew had been able to get out, but their dinghy was jammed in the wreckage. A rescue crew threw a Carley float over the side but it fell too far away from them: they couldn't see it, though the men on deck could see the fluorescent stain spreading out from the life jackets.

They stood helpless: half the crew of *Tracker*, and most of the squadron, including the Flying Officer who had sent those men out on the patrol. They stood as I had on the flight deck gazing at the three pinpricks that were their friends, who were waving back out of the Atlantic, even as *Tracker* wallowed away from them.

The ship stopped engines at once, *Tracker* pitching and rolling in her ungainly manner. She went astern, but in a rising sea they might lose sight of the men and run them down with the screws, or they might be thrown against the hull. So there was hesitation, and a first attempt to manoeuvre close enough to drop another Carley float was a failure, and still Moore on deck could only observe as the freezing aircrew drifted away again.

But this time, all three were rescued: a sloop and a rescue tug got to them. Two volunteers from the sloop wearing life-saving gear jumped into the water and got a hold on the observer and the air gunner, while the tug found the pilot. In the rough weather, there was no chance of transferring him back to *Tracker*; he spent the rest of the convoy idle in the tug.

*

Although there were plenty of scares and alarms, our return convoy had relatively little trouble from the U-boats. We spent much of our time in and out of the Operations Room just beneath the flight deck, where we were always welcome, the assumption being that the better informed we were, the better. There in Operations we saw the steadily changing plot of the situation, and the strategy that would have been inconceivable two years previously. Now, instead of attempting to dodge the U-boat packs, the convoys sailed straight at them, to bring them to battle and destroy them.

A year or two back, convoys had been pounced upon by eager packs of U-boats captained by ferocious and skilful young men: Otto Kretschmer, Joachim Schepke, and the remarkable Günther Prien who had sneaked through the defences at Scapa Flow and sunk the battleship *Royal Oak* at anchor, and got away with it. Otto Kretschmer had developed a tactic that for a while had completely bewildered the Royal Navy: he would surface his submarine right inside a convoy, and float there calmly shooting torpedoes at the merchantmen sailing by.

But by late 1943, all these famous aces were long dead: Prien's U-boat had been blown apart by depth charges; Kretschmer's boat had been forced to the surface and lashed with gunfire from a destroyer until, sinking, they had surrendered; Schepke's submarine had been rammed by a British destroyer, and as the ship's bow had rolled over the top of the submarine, Schepke, standing in the conning tower, had been crushed against the periscope.

The U-boat commanders were by now a great deal more wary, and although Admiral Dönitz continued to send them forth in some numbers, it was rumoured that more and more would turn tail and return to the concrete pens at Brest reporting some specious mechanical failure. They faced ever worsening odds. To begin with, they were more and more likely to be detected: the convoys now had scores of escorting warships such as Walker's *EG2*, and aircraft overhead also. If the U-boat dived, the escorts' ASDIC could detect a submerged U-boat a mile or more ahead, and with every day the ASDIC operators and designers understood more about factors such as deep layers of cold water that would alter the readings. If the U-boat surfaced, the latest Type 271 radar could pick out a conning tower in the dark or the mist. Then the hunt would begin, and those ships had formidable armaments, all designed for killing submarines. Where once they had released depth charges in patterns of five, Walker's sloops fired off ten at a time, able to sink hundreds of feet before they detonated, surrounding the submarines in a belt of crushing explosion. The destroyers had a new weapon called a 'hedgehog' fitted in the bows, that would fire a pattern of small bombs ahead of the ship even as it raced towards a submarine contact, to strike before the U-boat could slip away from the location.

Things were changing overhead also: now there were Catalina flying boats and Liberator VLR (very long range) patrols covering the former 'gap' in the middle of the Atlantic. The aircraft were equipped not only with radar but with Leigh lights, blindingly powerful searchlights. When they caught a submarine, they would drop acoustic homing torpedoes in her wake.

And all the time, our old Swordfish circled, with our eyes glued to the surface of the sea and the little glowing radar screen in front of our knees. Under our wings hung the armour-piercing rockets, or racks of anti-submarine bombs.

The *Kriegsmarine* had very little in answer to all this. Their torpedoes had magnetic fuses designed to pass underneath a merchantman and explode there, breaking the ship's back, but they often failed to explode at all, and simply continued out to sea on the far side. And while they were rushing to complete work on new

Schnörkel boats that could breathe underwater and travel fast, few of these had yet been delivered, and anyway the newer radar sets could often catch those too.

In one momentous encounter in May 1943, a pack of U-boats had closed in on convoy ONS 5, and for a moment it had looked as though the ships would be slaughtered. But thick fog had settled over the convoy. The U-boats had come to the surface, anxiously trying to find ships to sink but unable to see them. Two submarines collided and put each other out of action. The ships, though, had radar, and could see the U-boats. In one night, seven submarines were destroyed, and with them some 350 skilled crew.

It was rarely like that, of course: the usual experience of a Swordfish patrol was nothing to report, no satisfaction, no kill. Or there would be uncertainty. Sometimes the ASDIC contact would turn out to be a whale; it would still require investigation. We might glimpse a conning tower, see a long black shape diving below the broken sea, we might dive on it, fire rockets, drop depth charges, drop flares in the dusk and guide the sloops and destroyers to the site and watch as they unleashed their depth charges, circling the area dropping more for hours afterwards. But very often nothing came of it. Maybe there would be an oil slick, maybe not. Possibly the oil slick told of a U-boat drifting slowly, out of control, towards the bottom of the Atlantic. Possibly not. If we kept them away from the merchantmen, that was all that mattered.

No one on a convoy felt anything that you would exactly call sympathy for the U-boat crews, but with time my feelings about them altered and became more complex. In all the Battle of the Atlantic – which never let up from the very beginning of the war to the very end – some 3,500 Allied ships were sunk by the Germans and some 30,000 merchant seamen had lost their lives. That was very nearly the same as the U-boat crews who died. A number of German crews were captured, and we began to realize how extraordinarily young they were: even their captains were sometimes barely out of their teens. But then, we were young men too. Pete Pryor, our acting CO for a while, was at twenty-four positively old by 816 Squadron standards. In 1942, our average age in the squadron was twenty-one years and six months. By mid-1943 it had dropped to twenty years and three months.

We hated the U-boat men because they never rescued the crews of ships they sank – but then, how could they? There was barely enough room (or food, or water) in a U-boat for its own crew, let alone a dozen merchant seamen. We hated them for the stealth with which they approached the convoys, while coming to admit that they had extraordinary courage. By 1943, we were killing them far faster than they were killing us, and after the war it was realized that three in every four U-boat sailors had gone to the bottom with their boats, their 'iron coffins'. The strain that they underwent must have been appalling, both from fear of attack and depth charges squeezing them to death, and from the claustrophobia of the tiny space in which they lived. Most of a U-boat crew might be lucky to see the sky for weeks on end, while we could walk about on a wide open flight deck. In my *Manual of Seamanship* there was a paragraph about pumping fresh air into a submarine in an emergency. Imagine needing that.

But as we sailed among the convoys we were defending, we felt nothing like sympathy. I don't recall that we talked much about the U-boat crews, but I know I thought about them, and I hated them for (as I saw it) cowardly bastards. I would look at the entries in my code book, and in particular at a new one that I had added with a red pen:

514: U-boat damaged on surface. Crew attempting to surrender.

Why not just ram them and be done…

I developed a strange fantasy which, much later, I told to my son, and we found that we shared it. It was an idea of things sinking into very deep water, and of being able to see them as they went past. Perhaps it was Brian Bennett who started it, when he told me of seeing over his shoulder the bow of *Dasher* go down almost alongside him – so that I wondered what one would have seen had one been a diver deep below the surface? Imagine a submarine with a window in the bow, seeing a troopship that you had torpedoed, full of men and with its lights still burning, descending past you.

When I spoke with my son about this, he was a teenager and had recently been on holiday to Norway. There, on the Sognafjord, he had taken a small rowing boat from the hotel and had rowed out, looking at the far side of the fjord where the vertical rock wall of the mountains met with the waterline and seemingly continued vertically down beneath, without interruption (and without anything like a shore, or even a foothold for a sailor wrecked there). He had sat in his little boat and looked down into the water which, in places in the Sognafjord, is 4,000 feet deep. Then he had taken a coin from his pocket, placed it on the surface and released it, watching it slipping from side to side as it rapidly sank out of sight: how long would the coin take to reach the bottom?

As we talked about this, I remembered wondering how long a ship – or a shattered U-boat – would take to sink to the bottom of the Atlantic. Might any of the crew still be alive when they arrived? I would think about the very deepest seas: I now know that this is the Challenger Deep off the Philippines, though I don't suppose I knew it in 1943. Were there any submarines lying down there?

We wondered, my son and I, if somehow the water became thicker with depth and pressure, so that eventually at great depth you sank more slowly. From FAA aircrew who (like the original 816 Squadron) had trained in the Caribbean, I had heard of a curious thing: in Trinidad, they extract pitch from the ground, filling barrels with it. When cold, the pitch was as viscous and thick as could be, almost a solid. If you placed a coin on the surface – like my son's coin on the Sognafjord – it would just sit there, apparently unmoving. But after a while, it could be seen to sink, and would disappear into the sticky mass. Slowly, slowly, it would drop through the pitch and, after perhaps a year, it would reach the bottom; there, if you were able to turn the barrel over and open it, you might retrieve your coin.

So a submarine might go, very slowly, to the bottom of the Atlantic, with its crew frantically trying to save their lives. Even if one had no sympathy for the murderous cowardly bastards, it was a terrible thought.

A worse thought was a sinking Swordfish, dragged under by the weight of its engine, spinning slowly like a leaf as it drifted down.

*

When we were not flying our interminable circling patrols, we would try and amuse ourselves. We could drink astonishing amounts of very cheap liquor: whisky at 80 tots to £1, gin at 120 tots. But on an active escort carrier, heavy drinking (even supposing one's stomach could sustain it in those seas) was hardly encouraged, even by Freddie Nottingham.

We gambled: in retrospect I realize that we gambled a great deal. It was only for small sums, though the worse the weather and the greater the tedium, the greater the desire for excitement and the higher in consequence the stakes. We would sit in the Ready Room just under the flight deck, prepared to fly off at a few moments' notice, and we would play poker dice and cards for hours on end. John Moore recalled that there were big, comfortable armchairs in *Tracker*'s crew rooms – designed to give exhausted, oil-stained, unwashed, unshaven airmen a chance to relax – but that these chairs obliged you to loll backwards at an angle that made rolling dice awkward. So we would squat on the floor to play, and one Air Staff Officer reportedly said that we looked 'like a lot of thugs out of the Rake's Progress gambling in a graveyard' – or, as Moore put it, like the sweepings of a medieval jail.

We would play hockey on the flight deck; I was rather good at this, as we had played hockey on roller skates at Christ's Hospital school, hurtling about the concreted precincts. *Tracker*'s flight deck made an excellent pitch as long as you remembered to skip over the arrestor wires. We would use any old piece of thick, short timber as a puck, whacking it about with a walking stick. To get a game going was never hard; it was usually enough to pass through the various mess decks among the fitters or the air gunners, waving a stick and calling: 'Anyone for hockey-knockers?' Or it might be Seafires against Swordfish. One had to work a bit to keep the improvised puck from scuttling over the side of the flight deck, where it would land in the catwalk and possibly knock some unfortunate rigger on the head. But if it was going off the stern or bow, of course, one made no effort to chase it. There was no catwalk under *Tracker*'s bow, although with luck you might have landed in one of the gun-emplacements.

*

We returned to Scotland in late December 1943, just before Christmas, and there 816 Squadron parted company with HMS *Tracker*: the Admiralty had another carrier and another treat in store for us.

I have two photographs taken on board just before we disembarked. The first is of the interior of my untidy cabin (*plate 15*). On the open desk flap there is a turkey destined for my family. I must have kept it in the ship's chiller throughout the voyage.

The second shows our ebullient CO, Freddie Nottingham, in *Tracker*'s Operations Room discussing arrangements for a party somewhere in Soho or Mayfair: it is a proper squadron briefing and he has drawn a large 'how to get there' map of what looks like Piccadilly Circus (*plate 16*). And so we came ashore (*plate 17*).

We were smuggling, of course. You might have thought that HM Customs would be indulgent, given the perils that we had come through, but no. Our kit was frequently searched, and we'd be charged duty on the luxuries we brought home. These were not always what they are today: spirits, for instance, were far cheaper on ship than they were, for instance, in Halifax, Nova Scotia, where there was the added indignity of prohibition also – so the trade in Halifax was in selling our plentiful ration to the Canadians. But we wanted to bring home all the presents we could: silk and nylon stockings and anything else delectable and light. Much of this could be flown ashore in the Swordfish. Although Customs officers sometimes appeared at the airfields, they were never in time to meet us, and everything was long since concealed or deniable.

Such smuggled goods were known as 'rabbits'. The alleged origin of the term was a naval rating who had devised a complicated scam to get his goods ashore. He made two trips past the customs post, each time carrying a small wooden crate. On the first trip, the Customs man stopped him.

'What's in the crate?'

'Rabbits, sir.'

'Rabbits? Don't be cheeky, lad – open it up.'

'But they're wild, they'll escape.'

'Open it up!'

So the sailor had opened the crate, which really did contain a pair of wild grey bunnies brought with great care over the sea especially for this purpose. Given a prod from below, they gratefully leapt from the box and went scampering along the dockside causing splendid confusion as the chase ensued.

On the second trip shortly afterwards, the rating carried an identical crate, which he again declared to be rabbits – at which the Customs men impatiently waved him through. This time, the case was stuffed with silks and jewellery. Was the story true? I don't know, but ever afterwards we carried plenty of rabbits.

But I had a rather bulkier problem, not readily disguised as rabbits: the birdseed. It may not have been silk stockings, but it was contraband and dutiable nonetheless. Brian and Ken had their half a dozen leaky cardboard boxes to get ashore; I had my three large and bulging kitbags. I walked thoughtfully around our Swordfish and murmured to Bobby Creighton: 'Could we sling them from the bomb racks?'

He vetoed that notion: God knows what they would have done to his airworthiness.

'Besides,' he said, 'they might leak.'

We envisaged cruising above Prestwick with a trail of seed pluming into the sky behind us, pursued by open-mouthed gulls.

'Then they'll have to go inside.'

With considerable difficulty we packed the three kitbags into the rear cockpit. There was no room for George the air gunner.

'George, you'll have to catch the boat.'

With Bobby fretting about the addition of three hundredweight to our payload, and with me jammed uncomfortably between the sacks, we made it to shore. Ken, Brian and I took our bags and boxes, loaded them into the luggage van of the train and set off for Glasgow and London. From there we took a rather overladen taxi to Beckenham where the collection of valuable breeding budgies was soon to expire. The breeder had, in his backyard, a line of empty dustbins. He inspected our goods and happily pointed to the dustbins: 'Tip it in there, lads!'

Then he marched into his kitchen, fished in a desk drawer, pulled out a roll of banknotes and paid us on the spot.

I went straight to the branch of Martin's Bank where Gina again worked. We hadn't seen each other for months. She saw me come in, but had no chance to say anything, barely time to smile a delighted welcome as I sauntered up and nonchalantly dropped a roll of notes onto the counter before her.

'Put that into our account, darling.'

She picked up the money and counted it: £300!

'Where did you get it?' she asked in a rather frightened voice. She thought I had been engaged in privateering.

Notes

1. The Argentia base had been established in January 1941 and was fully commissioned that July. It was finally decommissioned in 1994.
2. The British press christened this 'the signing of the Atlantic Charter', but there was, in fact, no such single document signed at the time.
3. Two such USN 'K-ship' blimps out of Argentia made the first crossing of the Atlantic by non-rigid craft, in May 1944.

CHAPTER SEVEN
Chaser in the Ice

HMS *Chaser* was another escort carrier, built by Ingalls Shipbuilding at Pascagoula, Mississippi. Her keel was laid down in June 1941 as a merchantman but before her launch she had been requisitioned by the US Navy and conversion to an aircraft carrier begun, including from an early stage the fitting of British Type 271 shipboard radar. She was completed and handed over to the Royal Navy as *Chaser* in April 1943. She first sailed for active duty from Norfolk, Virginia, and joined convoy HX245 out of Halifax bound for the Clyde; although this convoy reached Britain without loss, an accident occurred on 7 July that was uncomfortably reminiscent of *Dasher* – an explosion in *Chaser's* boiler room.

She spent August and September under repair at Rosyth, on the Firth of Forth. On completion, *Chaser* embarked nine Swordfish and six Sea Hurricanes of 835 Squadron, heading for more Atlantic convoy defence – but again she broke down. No. 835 Squadron was disembarked, and *Chaser* went back into dock for mending. At last, in January 1944, she was allocated to us.

Chaser was no more elegant nor comfortable to sail in than *Tracker*. She looked very obviously like a merchantman minus her usual superstructure but with some 500 feet of decking perched on top (beneath which whistled the gales). Contrasting with the austerely bare expanse of the flight deck was the usual clutter clinging round the edges: small boats, derricks, fire hoses, netting, gun positions, Carley-floats and catwalks where men would gather to watch the flying. There was the familiar tiny bridge structure clinging to the starboard side: these bridges had to be small, both to prevent a lopsided weight and also to avoid being knocked off like a scab when the ship docked alongside a quay. Strung with a dozen wires and aerials and a flag or two, it looked like the drying green behind a tenement.

But on her first Atlantic crossing *Chaser* had carried with her something symptomatic of major changes in FAA lives: the aircraft on board were American, Grumman Avengers. These heavy, powerful planes were torpedo-bombers, though you might not have known it at first sight; unlike the poor old Swordfish, which flew with everything hanging out, on an Avenger the torpedo was carried in a neat enclosed bay. US naval aircraft design was moving ahead rapidly, though the same could not be said of the FAA. US planes such as Wildcat fighters had been flying from Scapa Flow since 1941; but only now was 816 Squadron to work with them.

Not that we gave up our Swordfish, however. The Stringbag's days as a torpedo-bomber were now well gone, but as an anti-submarine aircraft, able to fly from carriers in conditions that would have kept any other plane down in the hangar, she still had no equal. When we boarded *Chaser* in the Clyde, we had six stubby little Wildcats, all our Stringbags and some new ones too. We were *Chaser*'s first fully operational squadron.

In mid-February 1944 we sailed for Scapa Flow, taking the aircraft ashore at Hatston (Orkney) where they were all painted Arctic white. A convoy was preparing in Loch Ewe: JW57 consisted of forty freighters, two tankers and a rescue ship, bound for the Kola Inlet and Murmansk. It was, I believe, the largest convoy ever to make the Murmansk run. For 816 Squadron it was our second attempt to get to Murmansk, not having done so very well in *Dasher* (*plate 18*).

It was now some eighteen months since the disaster of convoy PQ17, in which two-thirds of the merchantmen had been sunk after the convoy mistakenly scattered. Things had changed. To defend JW57 there were six corvettes (all with their pretty flower names, *Bluebell, Camellia, Lotus*...) There were no fewer than a dozen destroyers,[1] and a force of cruisers in the background in case any larger German ship should decide to interfere. Only two months beforehand, *Scharnhorst* had done just that, sallying out from the Altenfjord to attack convoy JW55, and had been duly sunk by HMS *Duke of York* and her flotilla.

We also had two support groups from the Western Approaches with frigates and minesweepers, as well as a specialist anti-aircraft cruiser, HMS *Black Prince*. And then there was us, 816 Squadron in

HMS *Chaser* with our eleven radar-equipped Swordfish, and with our new Wildcats to give us some protection as we would be flying within range of German squadrons along the Norwegian coast.

It was well understood that fighter pilots were rather stupid and not very good navigators; unlike any decent Swordfish crew, they would almost certainly fail to find *Tracker* at sea. So Bobby Creighton and I were sent to meet the flight of Wildcats and to lead them back to the carrier. We were to rendezvous with them several hundred miles north of Scapa Flow.

It worked well; we met as arranged, their leader did his best to form up on us with the Swordfish trundling along at our best 85 knots, the Wildcats throttling back as best they could from their habitual two hundred. There was, as usual, strict radio silence, but aircraft in close formation had a crude means of communicating, called 'zogging': it was Morse code, done by raising and lowering one's forearm. I noticed that the Wildcat leader was trying to zog to me, but it was very difficult to read, he being in a small enclosed cockpit, I in a cluttered old Stringbag. His bushy black beard didn't help, so after a while I gave up. When we had both landed on *Tracker* and taxied forward of the safety barrier, he climbed out of his aircraft and walked back to meet me, pulling off his flying helmet.

'I see you don't recognize me,' he said. 'I'm Noel Simon – Christ's Hospital, Peel House B.'

At school I had sat opposite to him in the prep room, day after day.

'Good God, Noel, what a place to meet. Of course I didn't recognize you with that beard. Last I heard, you were working as a game warden somewhere in East Africa...'

I had more reason to be pleased a few days later.

This time we joined the convoy off the Faroes instead of Iceland. There was no point in pretending: we'd be spotted almost immediately. The convoy would have to steam almost the full length of the Norwegian coast, unable to move more than a few hundred miles offshore because of the ice of the Arctic winter pressing down from the north-west. Apart from the *Luftwaffe* fighters, the whole way up that coast we would be in range of shore-based bombers, let alone submarines and battleships lurking in any one of a thousand fjords.

And indeed, the Focke-Wulfe Condors found us on the second day, one of them making a wide circle almost all day. One of our Wildcats was flown off to chase it away, and at once we leaned of the risks of flying in the Arctic seas: the Wildcat attempted to attack the Condor, but at 5,000 feet its guns froze. Exasperated, the pilot brought the Wildcat back to *Chaser*; as he landed, the hook caught the arrestor wire and the jerk set the guns off, spraying the flight deck with cannon shells. By great good luck, no one was in the way.

Even the poor Swordfish were feeling the cold; most uncharacteristically, pilots were turning back to the carrier after short patrols with their oil pressure failed and engine temperatures soaring. No one had thought to bring Arctic grade oil, and in the air-coolers – which projected from the starboard side of the Pegasus engine – the oil was freezing. As usual, we solved this by the sort of makeshift expedient that a Swordfish could take in its stride. We had protective covers for the Pegasus engines; these would be wrapped around them when the aircraft were parked out of doors in the winter. We cut out the bits that covered the oil-coolers and strapped them in place over the working engines.

In case this wasn't enough, we broke a strict rule: the engines were started while the Swordfish was still sitting on the lift in the hangar space. This gave the Pegasus a chance to warm up and the oil to start circulating before being exposed to the cold. On this convoy we experienced temperatures down to minus 4 degrees Fahrenheit (36 degrees below freezing), and we managed to keep the Pegasus engines operating even then.

But the weather got worse. As we sailed north, snow squalls swept across the flight deck – but still we had to keep flying (*plates 19 and 20*). One Swordfish returned to *Chaser* in a snowstorm and hit the round-down stern of the flight deck, leaving its undercarriage there but slithering forwards to come to a safe stop – possibly the only occasion that a Swordfish managed to land without its undercarriage. Another day, a Wildcat crashed on deck. There was only one way to get rid of it quickly and clear the flight deck for other aircraft: the Wildcat had to be pushed over the stern of the ship. As the aircraft was about to plummet into the sea, an officer noticed a head bobbing about in the cockpit, and thought for a terrible moment that they were about to shove the pilot overboard also. The officer climbed quickly onto the wing, to find a rigger frantically trying to extract the aircraft's clock, regarded as a prize.

There was very good reason for all the urgency: supplied with good reconnaissance data from the FW Condors, packs of U-boats had assembled to await the convoy, in fighting groups named *Werwolf* and *Hartmut*. But when on 24 February the first of these surfaced to attack, they were immediately spotted from a Swordfish, which summoned HMS *Keppel*. The destroyer surrounded U-boat *U713* with depth charges, finishing it.[2]

On the 25th another U-boat was spotted from the air, this time from a long-range RAF Catalina flying boat, which dived on the submarine and released homing torpedoes that destroyed it. But the U-boats did not give up; during the short hours of daylight in which the Swordfish could fly, the submarines cruised just under the surface using their *Schnörkels*; then, when the light faded, they would surface and speed ahead, attempting to draw the convoy's destroyers and corvettes after them – in so doing, creating a high-speed signal from the ships' propellers that would provide the best targets for other submarines' acoustic torpedoes.

The German aircraft and submarines attempted to work together, the one spotting for the other, directing the U-boats to the kill, and trying also to keep the Swordfish off their backs. One afternoon, Bobby and I had made an attack on a submarine (I don't think we got it) when we were attacked ourselves by a German fighter-bomber. Behind me George the air gunner started firing back as the enemy passed over us (we were saved, again, by the Swordfish's ridiculously slow speed). But this was a terrifying situation: at any moment the German would turn and come back at our beam, with many machine guns to our one, which is just what he did… but a moment later a Wildcat came screaming down on him out of the cloud, and drove him off in a hail of gunfire.

As the Wildcat hurtled past us, I saw that it was my old friend Noel.[3]

It was all too dangerous for the submarines, with the swarming escorts by night and aircraft everywhere by day. No attacks were made on the merchantmen – but nor could we catch the U-boats. It became intensely frustrating; time and again either I, or George the gunner, or Bobby our pilot would spot the revealing feathering of a periscope, and bring the Swordfish round for a rocket attack, only to have the wary U-boat dive before our Swordfish (or the escort ships), lumbering into the blasting headwinds could reach it. We had no confirmed kills.

On the night of 25 February, however, the U-boats drew blood. In pitch darkness, *U990* twice torpedoed the destroyer *Mahratta*. Although two other destroyers went to her very quickly, *Mahratta*'s Lieutenant-Commander Drought and all but seventeen of his crew died in the icy sea.

For two more days we pushed north, the Wildcats driving the Condor reconnaissance planes back, while the Swordfish circled. The U-boats pestered the flanks of the escort and fired several GNATs (acoustic torpedoes) but without success. The first Swordfish patrols took off before dawn, to leave the convoy as little exposed as possible. We would make a point of beginning by circling low around the convoy to show ourselves to the merchantmen; otherwise their crews, especially the Americans, were inclined to loose off at anything in the sky (*plate 21*). The Wildcats were not risked on night patrols, but whenever conditions permitted – which is to say, as long as there was some visibility to enable the crew to glimpse a submarine and also to re-find *Chaser* for landing on – the Swordfish would fly at night also. Each patrol lasted somewhere between ninety minutes and three hours, and every one of us flew at least one patrol every twenty-four hours, often more.

*

When I think of the extreme conditions that we were flying in, and if I try to convey these, it is quite difficult even for me to believe everything that I recall. The mere fact of the Swordfish open cockpit in the Arctic is, in retrospect, almost incredible. Bobby, our pilot, was slightly protected by the wing almost above his head; George and I were both completely exposed.

Of course, we dressed up. We started with silk underwear, over which went oiled-wool long johns, then everyday cottons and a woollen battledress. In Arctic conditions we had a sort of teddy-bear outfit as well. Over that would go the Sidcot – an all-enveloping garment designed during the First World War and rather resembling a flannel 'unity suit' but in windproof gabardine, with huge pockets into which one stuffed maps and torches, navigation protractors, chocolate and the like. Under our leather flying helmet and goggles, we wore a woollen balaclava. Our flying boots were thick sheepskin. On our hands we wore heavy leather gloves with silk gloves underneath; I'd have to get the leathers off to do my navigation.

Our leather 'Irvine' flying jackets had, in theory, a provision for electrical heating, but we were told not use it: the Swordfish systems could not cope with three extra heating circuits for the aircrew.

To add to the discomfort, we had our safety harness which kept us strapped tightly in place, restricting circulation. One might have discreetly freed this or even taken it off, but the risk was considerable; during mine-laying operations in the channel, one Swordfish had encountered a group of German fighters, had taken wild evasive action – and the observer had been thrown out and killed.

The final discomfort was the never-properly solved issue of urinating. Some later Swordfish were fitted with a pee-tube that opened out under the fuselage; we could in theory do away with our improvised arrangements of funnels and bottles, although the pee-tube designers had not allowed for the swirling back-draft of the propeller that could send the pilot's urine in a fine spray over the air gunner. But in the Arctic, simply undoing the layers of garments, or finding a way out through them when shrunk to nothing by the ice, was beyond masculinity. Anyway, the pee-tube was almost certainly frozen up. We had little choice: we peed in our flying suits. For a minute or two there would be a pleasant warmth – then a growing chill, and then an acid chaffing that left us all with sore, red groins. If we managed to wash anything below decks in *Chaser*, getting it dry took superhuman patience; any warm piping was soon draped in underwear, gently steaming. Aircrew soon learned to carry as much clean underwear as possible on convoys. The one blessing of the American-built carriers in this respect was that they were equipped with plentiful hot showers; at least we could keep our skin clean, and prevent it from breaking down.

There was a further irony to all this: in 1940 the FAA had introduced the Fairey Albacore, another lumbering biplane but supposedly an advance on the Swordfish. As aircraft, Albacores were a failure: heavy, slow, with an unreliable engine, they were phased out well before the Swordfish they were supposed to replace. But in just one respect, Albacores were a leap forward: comfort. They had enclosed cockpits, nicely glassed in. They had windscreen wipers. They had heating. They had (as one pilot described it) a 'gentleman's toilet' which – there being less need for ten layers of clothing – was usable. But here is the irony: Albacores never served with the Arctic convoys.[4] They flew over the Mediterranean, and over the Western Desert of North Africa – theatres of war where an open cockpit might have been almost agreeable.

There were several journalists with convoy JW57, Father Divine's colleagues. After we had all reached home, one of them wrote an appreciative article for a newspaper in which he quoted Admiral Glennie heaping praise on *Chaser*'s Swordfish crews: 'They never let me down once, though they were so frozen that they had to be lifted out of the cockpits when they landed.'

And when we did land, we had to try and sleep in a cold ship heaving its way alongside the Arctic ice. Some tried to rest in the armchairs in the Ready Room, but even there you could be tipped out. Many of us found that, as on *Dasher*, the best option was to jam ourselves between the ship's steam piping – whether horizontal, vertical or somewhere between the two. Thus, at least, one had some warmth, and ran less risk of being dumped onto the steel cabin floor. But a deep and restorative sleep always eluded us.

In the face of such awful conditions, we had to fly off the heaving flight deck, to keep alert, to keep a sharp watch, to fight submarines and the *Luftwaffe* too, to make intelligent decisions, to navigate. To make the latter more difficult there was the white glare of the pack ice that we were skirting, and the wisping sea-smoke that blurred and confused the outlines of our own ships while concealing submarines. In February, the days were very short and the poor light and visibility day after day strained my eyes and my concentration. All the time, the three of us would have one ear attuned to the note of the Pegasus engine; the slightest falter or knock, real or imagined, would send a very cold sweat through us at the thought of the sea below.[5] At the end of a patrol, Bobby had to land us safely back on our carrier when he was exhausted and his concentration was ebbing away. It is a miracle that we survived – but not one aircrew was lost on that convoy.

When I wasn't flying, I was writing again:

> They had flown in the far north
> Down endless avenues, two hundred miles
> Of hanging gardens, snow squalls in clear skies
> Glinting in bright sun above black Arctic –
> Three minutes maximum survival time
> If the engine failed – but ravishing beauty
> That squeezed the heart, nevertheless.
>
> And at each cloud corner, the chance
> Of a lurking U-boat surprised on surface:
> Stalk it, hold breath attack from cloud
> Dive firing rockets screaming obscenities
> Die fuck you die sink sod you sink –
> Later, remorse and silent shame
> For this blood-lust staining the beauty.

*

On 28 February the convoy divided, one clutch of freighters heading into the frozen White Sea with two Russian ice-breakers, taking three more days to smash their way through to Archangel. The rest of us put into Kola Bay, and there the convoy's Commodore sent this signal:

To: Chaser   **From: Commodore**

[Thanks] from the whole of the convoy for your gallant defence. Your flying in this weather has been much admired by everybody.

To which Freddie Nottingham as Commander (Flying) got to make the reply for 816 Squadron:

> Thank you very much. Yours was the nicest signal we have ever received.

While the merchant ships went down into Murmansk itself, the Navy escort dropped anchor at Vaenga Roads, halfway up the inlet and some fifteen miles north of the port. There, if nothing else, we could sleep horizontally, lying in bunks that were oddly motionless. There, if nothing else, we found a supply of Arctic grade aero-oil. And an awful lot of snow (*plates 22 and 23*).

But really, there was little more besides a bleak military base with a small resident British staff; a substantial Royal Navy presence, including sloops and minesweepers working with the Soviet Navy to keep U-boats away from the harbour entrance; a large number of friendly Russians driving American military trucks that slithered dangerously across the docks; a small town that had been bombed to annihilation, and all that snow swathed over low hills and stunted little pine trees. The merchantmen were unloaded, their tanks and machinery and crates of ammunition stacked high on the quay, and in return cargoes of bulk materials and ballast. The Russian welcome was effusive; 816 Squadron was invited to a party to drink terrifying quantities of vodka at the Red Army airbase outside town, and the next day invited the Russians back to *Chaser* to drink comparable volumes of RN whisky (*plate 24*).

On 2 March, the convoy reassembled as RA57, and set off back up the Kola Inlet for the sea. It seemed often to have been the case that convoys returning from Russia had a more exciting time than on the way there. This is curious: the Germans' object, after all, was not merely to sink ships but to prevent supplies being delivered in the first place. But JW57 had fired up the enemy, and could expect an eventful passage home; packs of U-boats would be waiting outside Kola Inlet.

To begin with, the Soviet Navy cleared the way with a flotilla of destroyers and minesweepers chasing the submarines away. The convoy formed up with *Black Prince* the anti-aircraft cruiser and ourselves following in *Chaser* in the centre as before. We took a route for home that meant passing between North Cape and the inhospitable cliffs of Bear Island, then heading for the Faroes, running more or less parallel to the Norwegian coast.

For the first two days the weather was awful; we were swept by snow squalls and high seas; there was no thought of flying. If we felt sorry for ourselves in Swordfish, sometimes at least we felt pity also for the crews of the smaller ships, bashed about by the gales. The little 'Flower'-class corvettes in particular (with their pretty names), though they had been a mainstay of convoy defence for years, were almost as miserable in a gale as a Swordfish. They rolled as badly as an escort carrier: a full 80-degree roll (40 degrees to port, then a nauseating 40 to starboard...) was common. Heavy seas flooded in through the hatches which had to be opened to access ammunition for the guns as they engaged aircraft or surfaced submarines. Water would deluge into the mid-ships and everything would soon be soaked. If we had problems peeing in a Swordfish, that was no worse than using the 'heads' (toilet) in a 'Flower', for the little ships' piping drained directly into the sea, which could come straight up at your backside. Always overcrowded, the crew had nowhere warm to sleep, and would tuck themselves into any corner that offered a little shelter.

We were almost better off on *Chaser*.

On 4 March, the weather cleared partially and almost at once we were spotted by Ju88s and Condors. There was no doubt as to what the result would be. The submarines started to close in – and the Swordfish patrols resumed in spite of the conditions. The ship was often covered in ice; gun mountings froze, signal lights were draped in impenetrable white shrouds. To place a bare hand on any metal fitting was to risk being cold-welded into position, and ripping the skin off (not that we were ever much inclined to remove our gloves). At such temperatures, metal became brittle, and the tail wheels of aircraft would snap on landing. The deck crews were constantly at work shovelling away snow or chipping ice off equipment, or blasting the arrestor wires with steam hoses. Imagine flying a night patrol, and returning after a couple of hours to see the dim blue deck-lights of the carrier below you on which you were supposed to land – and wondering if the deck hands had done enough with their brooms and shovels and hoses to give you something better than an ice rink to return to. It was, quite simply, terrifying.

On the dusk patrol that day Brian, Ken (his observer) and Biff Vines (their gunner) were flying some fifteen miles astern of the convoy, passing through snow showers. At 2,000 feet the wind was blowing at perhaps 40 knots. Then, on the surface some 5 miles away, they saw a U-boat in a clear patch of weather. Brian attempted to creep up on the submarine by nipping from cloud to cloud – but just as they closed in, the U-boat saw them and dived, even as Brian fired his rockets. Did we all really scream obscenities as we attacked, as I state in my poem? Yes, I think so. But Brian never saw what happened to his rockets, whether they hit or not, because the scene was immediately whited out by snow.

Others were having similar adventures. Another of the day's signals across the convoy relates rocket attacks on submarines from that morning – three attacks before 9 a.m.:

To: Vice Admiral Destroyers   **From: Chaser**
Aircraft report one U-boat attacked in position 250zz16 at 08.20.
One certain hit two possible. U-boat submerged and was attacked by destroyers.
One U-boat sighted in position 187zz22 at 08.47. Offa [destroyer] homed to position of swirl.
One U-boat attacked in position 187zz22 at 0615, two certain hits, two possible, U-boat eventually finished by gunfire from Onslaught [destroyer] who took off survivors.

To: Chaser   **From: Vice Admiral Destroyers**
Well done. It is nice to read.

Freddie Nottingham reported that every one of us in *Chaser*'s Swordfish had spotted submarines that day. John Beresford's encounter (the 06.15 hours attack tersely noted in the signal above) was typical. He was flying the Swordfish patrol shortly after dawn. As they turned around the escort screen, John's air gunner, John Beech, saw a surfaced U-boat and they dived into attack, not with rockets this time but with bombs. The U-boat, caught unawares, nonetheless replied with a blizzard of flak – for the newer German submarines were now fitted with much heavier anti-aircraft weapons. Bill Laing, the observer, saw oil spreading on the water; they had damaged the U-boat, and they signalled to the nearest destroyer – *Onslaught* – which hurried in firing as it came, hitting the U-boat again and again, puncturing her hull all over. *Onslaught* came up in time to pick up the German crew as the submarine's commander scuttled his boat.

Brian and Ken had more hunting when the weather improved two days later, on 6 March. A feeble sunshine removed the mist from the surface of the sea, making it far easier to spot the thread-like trace of a periscope or *Schnörkel*. On the dawn patrol once again, Ken spotted (*plate 25*) a U-boat on the surface, just a few miles astern of the convoy. No gales or snow squalls this time: the morning was calm, the sea docile, the visibility excellent with thin stratus cloud at 2,000 feet, just enough for Brian to approach without being spotted; he took a bearing on the submarine, moved into the cloud, flew blind for a few minutes and then reappeared with the unsuspecting submarine sitting on the sea in front of him. He dived, firing his rockets in a 'ripple' – two at a time, instead of a salvo of eight. The second pair hit; the U-boat began to sink almost before the crew realized that they were under attack. Ken saw men in the water; Biff, the air gunner, signalled to the destroyer *Boadicea*, which hurried over and picked up a handful alive, just before they perished. There came another exchange of signals:

To: Vice Admiral Destroyers   **From: Chaser**
Aircraft report submarine sunk 095zz15. Survivors in water. Will confirm.

V.A.D. to Chaser
Stout work. You always were a good cricketer.

We always liked to find survivors; they were proof that we had killed their comrades and their boat – cricket of a sort. There was a comeback, though: that same day a U-boat eluded both us and the destroyers, and sent torpedoes into a merchantman, *Empire Tourist*, sinking her.

And now we had another problem: lack of wind. Even a

Swordfish needed wind over the flight deck for take-off. Our Mark IIs were heavier than ever, especially with the rocket launch-racks under the lower wings, the eight 60-lb rockets themselves, and the metal sheeting of the wing to prevent it catching fire when we shot the rockets. There was a partial technical solution: the RATOG, or rocket-assisted take-off gear, two faintly comical snouts projecting under the fuselage, with which the pilot could give us a few seconds of jet propulsion as we trundled along the flight deck (it worked surprisingly well). But RATOG could not throw us into the air on its own, and *Chaser*, even when steaming up the middle of the convoy, would often have to turn into the wind.

There was yet another difficulty: as ever, the most dangerous part of any patrol was the landing-on at the end. Again, one answer was to fly longer – and thus fewer – patrols. In order to achieve this, we needed more fuel, and in order to carry more fuel we dismissed our air gunners (George was not entirely sorry to be left behind), and replaced them with an extra fuel tank in the gunner's cockpit behind me. But an extra fifty gallons of fuel weighed a good deal more than George…

And now the sea was flat calm and there was no wind at all. Even with *Chaser* steaming flat out at 17 knots, a normally loaded Swordfish could not achieve sufficient lift to get clear of the sea; we would watch in dismay as aircraft trundled along the deck without so much as raising a wheel, and disappear over the bow of the boat – to reappear way below, frantically clawing its way forwards and upwards. It was hardly safe. So now Freddie Nottingham told us to do without either George or the extra fuel; we had to get airborne somehow. We took only half a tank, carried nothing more than two depth charges, and just managed to get into the sky and go looking for submarines.

But even this was not the complete answer, because it was not only submarines that we were fighting, but Ju88 bombers also. For the entire duration of the convoy, we were within easy striking distance of German bases in Norway – often only 100 miles from the coast – and the bombers were always there. That was why we carried our Wildcat fighters, but in the flat, windless calm, the Wildcats were even less able to get airborne than the Swordfish, which therefore had to fly against both submarines *and* bombers. No one wanted to fly with no defensive armament amongst well-armed Ju88s so, if there were bombers sighted, we would hurriedly summon the bemused air gunners and put them back into the Swordfish...

Such situations put a terrible strain on our CO, Freddie Nottingham, who, when not flying himself, must constantly – and seemingly without any sleep – be flitting between the bridge, the Operations Room, the deck and the hangar, assessing possibilities and giving orders for ever-more-dangerous operations to us, his friends and colleagues.

The strain on the squadron was recognized by the rest of the convoy and the escorts. At 12.55 on the 7th, there were more signals:

From: Vice Admiral Destroyers　　　　　　　　**To: Chaser**
I do indeed congratulate you and all under your command upon your plucky, cheerful and untiring offensive against German submarines. Thank you all.

Reply:
This has been our first operation and we have been trying our best to stage a good performance in front of so many small ship eyes. We are delighted that you think we have pulled our weight in the team. We would all like to thank you very much for such a charming signal.

Such sporting, almost schoolboyish courtesy among young men. Still, it mattered to us, even more so when, on the 8th, there came a signal from no less than the Commander-in-Chief of the Fleet:

When I visited you recently I thought *Chaser* would be a ship who could overcome any difficulty and strike hard. Now I know.

It was not over yet: *Chaser*'s 816 Squadron Swordfish attacked two more U-boats in one day. On 10 March, RA57 sailed back into the protective shelter of Loch Ewe and dropped anchor, and that would have been the end of the episode.

Chaser, however, did not go to Loch Ewe. As the convoy approached Scotland, it had divided and many of the escort had turned into Scapa Flow. There came an another signal from Sir Bruce Fraser who, just a few weeks beforehand, in the battleship *Duke of York* had sunk *Scharnhorst* when she had attempted to intercept another Murmansk convoy. Fraser now proffered an invitation to lunch with a cluster of naval dignitaries aboard his flagship.

Captain of *Onslaught* will be there too. You will enjoy it.
Barge will arrive for you at 12.15.

Instead of going himself, Freddie Nottingham sent four of 816 Squadron's triumphant aircrew (Brian and Ken, John Beresford and Bill Laing, his observer) with strict instructions to behave themselves.

Aware of the discomforts and privations facing the convoys, everyone did their best to relax and be sociable. Admiral Fraser decided to invite his Wren driver on board *Duke of York*. The girl demurred: she was not allowed to board without permission from her own commander. Astonished, Sir Bruce tried to order her onto his ship. Top Wren overruled him. To our great amusement, war broke out around the Scapa Flow anchorage, only to be concluded when another dinner party was held to which both Top Wren and Wren driver were invited. In the FAA we always felt that Wrens could be delightful until they were commissioned, after which demons of snobbery and toffee-nosedness got into them. No doubt they thought just the same of us.

Thus we enjoyed our triumph. In 1999 – fifty-five years later – my 816 Squadron friend Vic Smith sent me a copy of a letter he had received. It was from a former merchant seaman whose attention had been caught by something Vic had written and published in a newspaper.[6] The letter said that this man had been one of the crew of a freighter in that convoy, JW/RA57, and he was writing to offer Vic and the rest of us his thanks for having saved his life.

Unfortunately, we couldn't save poor *Chaser* from humiliation…

We flew 816 Squadron's Swordfish to Donibristle on the south coast of Fife for thorough maintenance, suspecting that the poor-quality oils that we had been using, the high resulting engine temperatures and perhaps the fearfully low air temperatures also might have taken their toll on the Peggies. Such unworthy doubts: when the engineers stripped down all the engines, they could find no excessive wear at all. So, back to Scapa Flow, expecting to be given a short leave and then to join the next Arctic convoy.

On 13 March, we lay at an anchored mooring in Scapa Flow, still patching ourselves up (*plate 26*). We laundered our reeking, urine-stained clothing, and repaired torn code books and charts. We wrote letters and sent them off in handfuls. We ate hot meals and took hot showers. We walked on solid ground, before returning to a ship that was almost as motionless. We thought back over what had happened in the last fortnight, and offered quiet thanks for our survival. We received more congratulations. We went to the wardroom bar and we drank, and now felt few inhibitions about drinking deep.

Chaser too was having her engine stripped down and her boilers cleaned, for the pounding that ships sustained in the Arctic gales put a fantastic strain on them. So, apart from auxiliary generators, the carrier was without power and unable to get under way.

Another gale began, sweeping across the Scapa Flow anchorage. The winds struck *Chaser* beam-on – and, like all the escort carriers, *Chaser* presented an enormous, high beam to wind and sea. As the gale increased, she began to drag the anchors of the mooring. We could not start the turbines (they were in bits), nor were there any tugs in sight. The more the anchorings shifted, the looser they became and the faster we moved. I have a vivid recollection of standing out on the flight deck with the rest of the squadron, watching in horror as *Chaser* seemed to bear down, broadside on, upon the entire Home Fleet, with men rushing about their ships in alarm. Goodness knows what frantic signals were flashing between the bridges of the ships, but what could anyone do? First in our line of fire was our own sister ship, the carrier *Attacker*...

But before we actually hit her, we ran aground.[7] We were on the rocks. We lay there in the middle of the Flow with *Chaser* at a severe list, steep enough to make walking across the wardroom to the bar an awkward uphill climb (*plate 27*). It wasn't really *Chaser*'s fault, but nonetheless it was most embarrassing. I doubted that we'd be getting more lunch invitations to the *Duke of York* in a hurry.

*

We were due for some leave, badly overdue. If there was one thing to be said for the gale that grounded poor *Chaser*, at least it saved us from a second Russian convoy.

I had arranged to meet Gina in Arbroath, where we were to spend some time with the family of Ernie Myles, the church warden with two lovely daughters who had welcomed my New Zealand friend Murray and me during our training. That, at least, was the plan; Gina took the night train and came to Scotland, waiting for me at the Myles home. I didn't turn up; I was shipwrecked, and had no way of either reaching her or communicating: a shipwreck was information that came under the Official Secrets Act. Eventually, we were able to get a boat ashore, and fly from Hatston to Edinburgh from where I telegraphed Gina to return to London, without being able to say why.

After some ten days' leave, the squadron reformed. Our old Stringbags were pronounced fit for further service – though we had no carrier. How could we sail again to Murmansk? We never did. A quite different order came through: we were to go south, to Cornwall. In the English Channel, something very different was about to happen.

Notes

1. One of these was HMS *Wanderer*, commanded by another successful submarine-hunter, Bob Whinney, who wrote his own account of anti-submarine warfare in the Atlantic and Arctic and in particular this convoy, JW57. The book is entitled *The U-Boat Peril* (1986). It is perhaps a measure of the continued disregard of the regular RN for the FAA that, although Whinney himself had fought hard to get anti-submarine tactics taken seriously by the Navy, his book makes almost no reference to the Swordfish patrols, nor mentions the presence of any aircraft carrier.

2. Another destroyer that raced to this attack was HMS *Wanderer*, commanded by Bob Whinney. *Wanderer* was ordered to back off, leaving Whinney 'speechless with rage' (his words).

3. Noel Simon became a distinguished natural history writer, with forty books to his credit, as well as a wartime mention in despatches.

4. Albacores did, however, take part in the defence of Norway, and in particular the strike in July 1941 launched from the carriers *Furious* and *Victorious* against German units in the Norwegian harbours at Petsamo-Kirkenes. It was a sad failure. Very little was achieved by the attack, and large numbers of aircraft were lost.

5. The FAA pilot Terence Horsley wrote: 'There was much to be said for the policy of a well-known lady pilot who, on her celebrated long-distance flights, used to paste a sheet of paper over the oil-pressure gauge before she crossed the open sea.' (*Find, Fix and Strike* 1944). He was presumably referring to either Amy Johnson or Amelia Earhart.

6. Vic Smith had been a midshipman in 816. He and Robert shared a taste for English literature, and Smith had become a newspaper editor in Birmingham.

7. Some sources suggest that *Chaser* did actually hit *Attacker*, but aircrew accounts do not confirm this.

CHAPTER EIGHT

Channel Firing

There was to be an invasion of France; we didn't know when, but preparations were being made on both sides of the Channel. The planners on the English shore believed that the invasion fleet and also the supplying convoys could be beset by U-boats[1] and E-boats (fast torpedo boats) coming from Brest and the other ports of occupied France.

Once again (as at Thorney Island and Exeter in previous years), 816 Squadron was loaned to RAF Coastal Command, and we flew our Swordfish far to the south-west, to Perranporth in North Cornwall, from where we were to fly night patrols over the Channel approaches and all along the northern coast of Cornwall, from Hartland Point down across Newquay and Penzance and on to Wolf Rock, stuck out in the sea beyond Land's End.

We went without Freddie Nottingham; he was sent to take command of a carrier squadron in the Pacific, and we missed him sorely. In his place came a Royal Navy officer, Lieutenant Commander Peter Snow, a pleasant but somewhat ineffectual chap who would freely admit that we knew far more about the job than he did.

Not that we knew nor were told much about what was going on. From the air we could see vast amounts of shipping in the English Channel and the Bristol Channel, and rumours of all sorts of deceptions circulated.[2]

Having been Arctic white, once more the Swordfish were painted black; they again looked faintly sinister. We received new equipment, including a much improved altimeter, radio-controlled. This was a relief. Our previous altimeters had been barometric: they took a pressure reading at take-off and compared it with the reduced pressure at altitude thereafter. But in the course of a three-hour flight the weather (and the barometric pressure) might well change. We recalled the mine-laying in poor weather we had done from Thorney Island: one didn't want to be at the wrong height when quietly placing a mine in Cherbourg harbour, or when skimming home over the sea, but it had happened. We remembered the returns in the fog, the scary landings at unfamiliar south coast airfields that we could barely find, always with the steep flank of the Downs nearby; it would be nice to be sure of our flying altitude. I recalled my good friend Jock Douglas; if we had had decent altimeters in 1942, Jock and his pilot would not have flown into the Portsdown Hills and been killed.

We received new ASV radar as well, now supposedly accurate to within 100 yards: this, with its ability to read the landscape in front of us, might also save us from flying into the cliffs of our homeland.

Again, we were armed with rockets, but also with a new device called a 'glow-worm', which was a rocket coupled to a parachute flare. In addition to the dive-bombing of submarines, we were now back to tactics that we had learned seemingly so long ago. Again, we practised the glide bombing of E-boats. We practised flying in close formation at wavetop height, and in particular we practised dive-bombing wooden targets floating on the sea.

The common image of Second World War dive-bombing involves either a Japanese kamikaze plunging into the superstructure of an American warship in the Pacific, or a Stuka similarly plunging upon panicky horse-drawn artillery on the roads of France (as in my early poem, p.51). In both such images, the aircraft screams down upon its victims in a near vertical drop. Dive-bombing in a Swordfish was never quite like that; a Swordfish was far too ladylike to scream at anyone. We would form up in line astern and approach our wooden practice-target bobbing about in the Bristol Channel, towed behind some superannuated minesweeper or tug, then the aircraft would drop on it one by one in a dive between 60 and 65 per cent before releasing the bomb and hauling away. It was a very peculiar sensation, seated in a diving biplane in that open cockpit. Bobby Creighton in front of me at least had the notion of being in control. All I could do was to cling on to the sides of the cockpit to steady myself and thank heavens for the safety harness that stopped me slithering to my death. Behind me, George the gunner – who faced the rear – was more or less lying on his back, without being able to see what was going on. It took some getting used to.

The Swordfish was patiently reassuring, and so steady in the controls that it was possible for Bobby to hold the dive down to just a few hundred feet before hauling back on the stick. Even weighing three-and-a-half tons and nose down, she still fell slowly, the airspeed indicator never exceeding 200 knots even if you tried hard. There was a problem here: low speed might have reassured the aircrew, but it vitiated the attack. 200 knots was only just fast enough; the effectiveness of the armour-piercing bombs depended on their smashing through the decking of a ship with as much impact as possible, so that ideally a dive attack would start at 14,000–15,000 feet with the bomb released at around three thousand. The lower you started, the lower the release, the less the impact. At much this time (April 1944), the *Tirpitz* was dive-bombed in a Norwegian fjord by FAA Barracudas. The great battleship was struck by fourteen direct hits and should have gone straight to the bottom – but the bombs had been dropped from around 1,000 feet and, of all those fourteen bombs, not one penetrated her armoured lower decks. Although badly damaged, *Tirpitz* did not sink.[3]

So we clambered up as high as we could before diving: a Swordfish couldn't climb higher than 10,000 feet anyway. And then we plunged. Bobby and the other pilots liked to leave their bomb release till the last moment, so as to improve their accuracy, but if we were too low, we stood a good chance of being blown apart by our own bomb detonating below us.

We practised and patrolled, and patrolled and practised. We grew bored and tense. At least it was summery, most of the time. We flew by night, but by day we had the long sandy beaches of North Cornwall where we could doze and swim (*plate 28*). These beaches had been heavily wired up earlier in the war, to prevent German landings, but after D-Day the wire was removed. We made good use of surfboards belonging to the cliff-top hotel that had become our quarters,[4] and discovered also enormous shellfish: no one had been to collect them for several years. I had a new friend in the squadron: John Godley (the future Lord Kilbracken) was tall and raffish with a diffident grin, and was always ready with scabrous jokes. Life could have been quite pleasant in its way – if you could ignore the frustrations.

Gina, though, was in some danger, and felt that I ought to have a taste of that.

At Perranporth we were a long way from the menace that was now afflicting the south-east of England: the buzz-bombs. The V-1 was just a tube with wings on, a jet engine with a limited supply of fuel mounted at one end and a large amount of explosive at the other. They flew at between one and two thousand feet making a continuous farting sound until they ran out of fuel. The motor stopped, the noise cut off suddenly and the aircraft-bomb just plunged nose-down into the ground and exploded, devastating everything around it. Everybody on the ground within a wide radius heard them coming and heard when the motor stopped. They then had a terrified wait for the explosion, taking cover if they could reach it in the next half minute or so.[5]

Gina – still working at Martin's Bank in the City – was staying with her father in Eltham. Their house was damaged by a near miss early in the buzz-bomb campaign, the windows blown out. She sent me a telegram in Cornwall, with the result that I was given some leave to go up to London for a few days to help repair the damage. I rather resented being snatched from my peaceful battle zone into the dangerous civilian zone. One afternoon in London, thinking that I was alone in the house I decided to have a bath. As I lay gently soaking, I heard one of those wretched bombs approaching – and then its engine stopped. Gina's father had had a 'Morrison shelter' (like a very strong steel dining table) installed under the stairs; that was the place to be. I leaped out of the bath, grabbed a towel and scampered wet and naked downstairs to throw myself into the shelter – only to find it rather crowded: her father was already in it.

The bomb overshot us and landed in a field at the bottom of the road. By then, this being the 1940s, I was more concerned with my embarrassment than with my survival.

Buzz-bombs were succeeded by V-2 rockets;[6] these gave no warning at all, nothing but a sudden bloody great explosion, literally out of the blue. When the first few landed, the government's propaganda machinery tried to defuse panic by spreading stories of gas mains exploding. I was glad to get back to the safety of Perranporth.

*

But the atmosphere continued tense and uneasy. The weather was often poor, never mind the summer, and while the RAF in all their fearsome modern Beaufighters and Mosquitoes might be grounded, still we flew our Swordfish. Never mind the new altimeters and ASV: we hated it. A story went round about two Swordfish with another squadron who had been flying a night patrol and who had been caught by thick fog on their return. They both realized that they had no option: they had to make a forced blind landing before their fuel ran out. They descended as slowly as they could, throttled right back so that they drifted earthwards at just 55 knots (as only a Swordfish could), unable to see the ground beneath them and with no idea whether they were heading straight for a power cable, a building or a ravine. By complete chance, they both came down in a field, wrecked their undercarriage but climbed out alive. It was all very well, but anything other than Swordfish wouldn't have been flying at all.

John Godley, in his own account of that time,[7] relates returning to Perranporth in heavy cloud with the RAF controllers assuring him that visibility was excellent, until his air gunner radioed down to them: 'Put your heads out of the window!'

And all to what end? Still we knew little of what was happening. We chased a few E-boats (they always got away). We tried to keep cheerful. John had taken a cottage in Perranporth village, and we would retreat there to eat and relax with him and his wife, Penny, when we could, but we were not allowed to go any further from the aerodrome in case there was an emergency.

A letter arrived, and was duly pinned to the notice board in the wardroom (I saved the letter, and have it now in my photo album). It was from Dwight D. Eisenhower:

Soldiers, Sailors and Airmen of the Allied Expeditionary Force! You are about to embark on the Great Crusade, toward which we have striven these many months... The

tide has turned! The free men of the world are marching
together to Victory!

When it came, we missed it. The first I knew of the D-Day landings
was when my steward brought me a cup of tea in the morning and
put it down saying 'Congratulations, sir!'

'What for?'

'It's all on the radio, sir. You were there, weren't you?'

Well, yes, we'd been chasing E-Boats the night before. We hadn't
known that they were actually looking to attack the invasion fleet
that was sailing just then, and as usual we hadn't caught any. So
much for my part in the reconquest of Europe.

For the next few weeks our patrol patch moved steadily south
across the Channel, as on the ground the invasion force moved
down the Cherbourg peninsula. The Stringbags must have made
some of the American forces think that they'd shifted back a war.
We did manage some rocket attacks on the E-boats from around
1,000 feet. After a time we were given one specific target: it seemed
that some important German units were trying to escape from near
Cherbourg heading in E-boats across to the coast of Brittany, to St
Malo, to the Channel Islands or to the U-boat pens of Brest. We were
supposed to try and intercept them – but it was a forlorn task, and
we never spotted our target. On a couple of occasions, returning
past my ancestral home of Guernsey, we were fired on by our own
anti-aircraft batteries. It made me very indignant, while Bobby
seemed to think that it was my personal responsibility and that I
should do something about it.

As the invasion moved further and further inland, the
contribution that 816 Squadron could make seemed more and more
puny. After all our ordeals protecting convoys, we suddenly
seemed redundant. Morale sagged. Moreover, some of us were
becoming 'twitched', wondering when our luck would run out.
John Godley realized that – after years of gung-ho missions – he
had begun to lose his nerve, and had started bringing his aircraft
back from patrols early, with feeble excuses about the weather and
low oil-pressure in his engine, things he would have blithely
ignored a year before.

Others had doubts about Peter Snow, the new CO. He was said to be a poor pilot, or at least an inexperienced one compared with the rest of the squadron. Perranporth airfield was positioned high above the coast, with a dangerous up-draft of air lifting the aircraft as you approached over the steeply rising ground, only to suddenly dump you as you were about to land. Snow seemed to judge this badly, and his crew became more and more twitched to the point that his observer refused to fly with him, and the air gunner reported for a patrol drunk, and muttering, 'What the hell, he's going to kill us all anyway.' Another young aircrew, against all the regulations, took off one day with a local girl stowed on board, and were soon in very serious trouble.

We were beginning to feel mutinous.

By day we were still more or less confined to the airfield and our quarters in the nearby former hotel, though we were allowed to go far enough afield to play a local school at cricket. In the hotel there remained a bar billiards table; you had to put a sixpence through a slot at one end to activate it, and the sixpences were counted by a little device like a bicycle milometer that clicked one digit at a time. We managed to detach this from the under-surface of the table, and invented a pastime that consisted of seeing how many digits a minute each of us could move it on with an index finger. Competition became fierce; we sat around clicking like mad and calling out the scores.

Then there was the cuttlefish: another symptom of our moral decay. As so often, it was a Ken Horsfield enterprise. Two or three of us were walking along the beach one sunny afternoon. Ken kept picking up pieces of fish-bone with which the beach was strewn, and examining them closely.

'Do you know what this is?' he asked.

'Decayed cod-fish, by the smell,' someone replied.

'No, it's cuttlefish. Cage birds love it. They sharpen their beaks on it. Can't get it for love nor money in the trade. And look at this beach – covered in it.'

We set about collecting it, and stored it in a kit bag in Ken's bathroom. The marketing was Ken's province, but it soon became urgent: the smell was becoming overpowering. He had to tip it all into the bath and wash it, then dry it – but in the meantime the stewards began complaining to the CO who ordered Ken to get rid of it. By this time he had put a small ad in his favourite periodical, *Cage Birds Monthly*, offering it for sale at three shillings and sixpence a pound: 'Send a postal order to Sub Lieutenant Horsfield, c/o 816 Squadron, Royal Navy'. He actually managed to sell one pound of his cuttlefish before the reek got the better of us and we rebelled; we forced him to close down, taking the whole collection down to a cave near the hotel and dumping it.

Meanwhile, our frustration grew; we were wasting time, doing nothing, taking risks flying to no purpose. We became short-tempered and foul-mouthed; recently, at my son's request I compiled a list of the swear words we used when trying to find a carrier in mid-ocean, or Perranporth airfield in the fog. In spite of the instruction to drop the 'very lower-deck' word *fuck* from our officer's vocabulary, it was, of course, used in abundance and in every possible combination with *hell*, *Christ*, *Jesus* and *shit*, qualified by *bloody*, *bleeding* and *sodding hell*. Nothing unfamiliar there, but there were also the period pieces: *Heaven alive!* was common, as were *Shitty death! Jumping Jesus! Hell's bells! Holy mackerel!* (Why mackerel? Why not sturgeon?)

We were sick to death of night patrols. I wrote a new song, and the whole squadron would roar it out at the piano, to the tune of 'John Brown's Body':

> Let's get back to sea again and catch up on our sleep,
> Let's get back upon the bosom of the rolling deep,
> Let's get back to sea again and get our piss-ups cheap,
> For we're chocker with patrols from Perranporth!

Perhaps as a result of the meter-twiddling competitions, the cuttlefish and this song, Peter Snow at last took action.

A stranger appeared among us, apparently an officer, but one who seemed to do nothing but sit around watching; we were watching him too. Not knowing who he was, we reported to Peter that the man was suffering from operational strain – to which Peter replied: no, it was us showing the strain. Peter had reported to the Admiralty that he thought the squadron was in poor shape and should be disbanded. The stranger had been sent to investigate: he was a surgeon-psychiatrist.

And he had agreed: we were indeed to be disbanded. It was the end of 816 Squadron, 'my gang' for more than two years; I would lose Bobby and George also. I was the longest-serving officer in the squadron, having been with 816 since its reforming at Lee-on-Solent in May 1942.

For our reunion dinner in 1991, Don Ridgway drew up a balance sheet of what the squadron had lived through. Admitting that it was impossible after nearly five decades to be fully accurate, he nonetheless worked through his own logbook and extrapolated from his knowledge of how many aircraft we had had: six to begin with, fifteen at the end. He concluded that we had flown 855 operational sorties, of which some 87 per cent were against U-boats. The usual U-boat watch averaged about three hours, so we had probably flown around 180,000 miles at a cruising speed of 85 knots. Since we surveyed (visually, or by radar) a corridor some twenty miles wide, we could claim to have watched over not much less than four million square miles of the North Atlantic and Arctic oceans.

What had we achieved? Twenty-one U-boat sightings, with three definite kills, three probables and three possibles – which is to say, perhaps 450 young German sailors killed or captured. We could also claim to have kept very many more submarines under the surface. Three of those, Johnnie Walker's sloops had then sunk. The others had only seldom got to fire torpedoes at the ships in the convoys, and that was the real point. We had escorted one of the largest convoys ever to reach Murmansk, with the loss of one destroyer on the northward run and one merchantman coming home. Apart from these, no merchantman or escort had been sunk on any of the convoys we had protected either in the Arctic or the Atlantic – which meant hundreds of ships.

What of the cost, though? Never mind the Stringbags, said Don: they were meant to be expendable. They could be cannibalized and reassembled from bits, but you couldn't do that with young men, aircrew and troops. Any victories we claimed had to be set against ninety-seven lives, average age perhaps twenty-three.

*

At the beginning of August 1944, one by one and in the light of operational experience, we were interviewed as to what we would like to do next. I said, emphatically, that I wanted to get back on a carrier, even if it was just a little converted freighter pottering across the Atlantic – I didn't care what. When I said that I wanted to join such a vessel, the interviewer from the Admiralty was rather taken aback, pointing out that I was well due for resting from operations. But he agreed at last, and gave me a posting that would take me back into convoy escorts.

Why on earth had I done this? After surviving so much, why put myself back in the line of torpedo fire and watery death? Well, it was the cuttlefish suggested it. I was mercenary: Gina and I needed the money. I envisaged further convoys to Halifax, further consignments of birdseed, plus my extra pay saved up while at sea. Besides which, Perranporth had got me down badly; I longed to get back on a carrier. I wasn't the only one: John and many others in 816 Squadron asked to do the same.

There's a photograph of the squadron taken at Perranporth on 1 August 1944, just one week before we were disbanded; it's a farewell portrait. I'm not in it; Jumbo Kay and I had been sent to fetch spares from a neighbouring aerodrome: we had been reduced to gofers. Judy is there, Ken Horsfield's dog, seated massively in front of Peter Snow, the commander who had ordered our dissolution and who looks rather buttoned-up. John is there in the front row, his cap askew at the louche angle he generally wore it, and his appealing look of bashful raffishness instantly recognizable. Bobby is there in the front row, looking slumped and tired. Standing behind John is the only man with a beard: Ken, the dauntless entrepreneur. In the third row is George, grinning cheerfully. But as a group, we look stiff, unsmiling, uncertain quite how to present ourselves, now that we'd been declared unfit as a unit. Behind us, above the protecting earth embankment of the aircraft dispersal, rises the massive top wing of a Swordfish, one tip of her propeller just visible.

A few of the squadron had flown themselves to near exhaustion, and were firmly taken out of front-line duties: Don Ridgway became a navigation instructor; Brian Bennett was to be a deck-landing tutor – for which, having made over one thousand landings himself, he was more than qualified. But in August 1944 the rump of 816 Squdron flew north to Maydown, near Londonderry in Ulster, the base of 836 Squadron into which we were to be absorbed. We were going back to sea again, to catch up on our sleep.

Notes

1. Johnnie Walker, the celebrated U-boat hunter from the North Atlantic convoys, organized protection for the invasion fleet. No U-boat ever made a successful attack.
2. See the discussion in the Introduction regarding Operation *Mincemeat* (p.10).
3. But she never put to sea again either. At the end of the war, *Tirpitz* was still skulking behind torpedo booms and under camouflage nets.
4. 1944 seems an early date for surfing in the UK, but the Museum of British Surfing confirms a number of mentions of service personnel surfing during the war, especially in Devon and Cornwall. My thanks to them. Don Ridgway, however, has no recollection of there being any boards available, saying that the swimmers just lay themselves down.
5. V-1 bombs killed nearly 23,000 people, mostly in London and the Netherlands, almost all of these civilians.
6. Although terrifying, V-2 rockets were less effective than the V-1. They buried themselves before exploding, and thus the damage caused was restricted: they killed some 7,000 people. They were also very expensive to build, and were a serious drain on the remnants of Germany's war economy.
7. *Bring Back My Stringbag* by John Godley, Lord John Kilbracken (1979).

CHAPTER NINE

Down, and Out

In the weeks before D-Day, a group of new Swordfish crews had joined us at Perranporth to bring us up to strength. Some of these had come from 836 Squadron, and we now returned to 836 with them. No. 836 Squadron was an unusual group: it was, to begin with, by far the UK's largest, with ninety crews and a similar crowd of Swordfish. Why so large? Well, 836 was the 'Mac-ship' Squadron, scattered between a score of makeshift aircraft carriers.

Mac-ships were, in retrospect, a remarkable phenomenon. Like *Dasher*, *Tracker* and *Chaser*, they were at heart freighters. But their conversion was even more rudimentary, for while operating as aircraft carriers they were also still functioning cargo ships: hence the 'Mac' in most of their names, for Merchant Aircraft Carrier. Whereas the holds of *Tracker* (for instance) had been adapted to contain a hangar for the Swordfish and Wildcats, plus all the workshops, fuel stores, magazines, showers, cinema and sickbay, mess decks and berths for several hundred men and two dozen aircraft, Mac-ships had a wooden flight deck, but no hangar and no lift. A handful of Swordfish – generally just three or four – lived permanently up on deck, lashed down in the gales. All refuelling, re-arming and repairs took place right there in the open. Meanwhile, cargoes that could be pumped or blown – fuel or grain usually – were loaded or offloaded out from under the sides of the flight deck.

The Mac-ships were an emergency stop-gap measure devised when the Battle of the Atlantic was at its height in 1941 and early 1942. Many were built, with names often beginning *Empire Mac*.... Being relatively small ships (generally c.8–10,000 tons), they could be put together at speed[1] in civilian yards that normally only built tramp steamers, and fitted out to rather lower merchant standards. They were only used for the North Atlantic; being even smaller and more ungainly than escort carriers like *Chaser*, they would have been worse than useless in the ferocious Arctic seas, and would quite likely have foundered.

Mac-ships were slow – sailing at only 10 or 11 knots – but then convoys were very often slow. The Mac-ships were crewed by merchant seamen, together with a detachment of defensive gunners, ourselves and our fitters, all now carrying Merchant Navy paybooks and under the discipline of a civilian captain. It felt very different. Once at sea, the little group of aircrew and fitters had to be entirely self-sufficient, and provided for ourselves all the skills normally found in the far larger company of an escort carrier.

The enormous 836 Squadron, based at Maydown in Northern Ireland, was a pool serving the Mac-ships – nineteen of them, one flight of aircraft per ship. John was told he'd be with the *Adula*. I was assigned to the *Empire MacCabe*,[2] which beneath her flight deck was an oil tanker (one would have preferred not to be on an oil tanker; they tended to attract U-boats). At Maydown I met the new pilot I'd be flying with: Dave Wormald. He was a very good pilot, as he needed to be, for the flight deck of a Mac-ship was as small as that of an escort carrier, little more than 450 feet long and 62 feet wide. To put us safely down on that little space as the ships pitched and rolled in the Atlantic required all Dave's considerable skill and nerve. Mind you, he was lucky to get me as an observer.

We escaped from Maydown whenever we could; I still have a postcard I sent to Gina from the beauty spot of Castle Bridge, Buncrana, in Donegal. *Here for a very pleasant weekend...*

John Godley's ancestral home, where his wife and baby boy waited, was a few hours' drive over the border to the south. His parent's house at Killegar was a crumbling mansion, designed like Blenheim Palace by Sir John Vanbrugh but not quite so well maintained. I remember visiting it again after the war: there was no electricity, half the rooms were uninhabitable, water poured in through the roof if it rained and one spent the night patrolling the corridors with buckets and enamel basins to catch the drips. By day there were eels to be fished from the twin lakes, which could be hung from the roof down the living room chimney to smoke over the peat fires. The family struggled to make an eccentric lifestyle pay. They once did a deal with Fortnum & Mason in London to supply cream cheese blended with Guinness, but it all went horribly wrong: the first batch was returned, containing something nasty and decaying. At some point in the process the cheese had been warmed in a pot over the fire – but up above, an eel had previously become lodged in the chimney, where it had eventually rotted and fallen...

Killegar was a very long way from a Swordfish on a rolling deck, though similarly makeshift.

The squadron sailed, dispersed among our respective Mac-ships. In August 1944, in the *Empire MacCabe* I plodded slowly across the Atlantic, confined to daytime patrols: our ship was too small and was not equipped for night flying. Indeed, we were barely equipped for anything; the only shelter the aircraft or the troops had when working on repairs was a row of palisades along the sides at the bow, enough to break the force of the gale a little. The weather took its toll as ever. On *Empire MacAlpine,* they lost all three of their Swordfish to storm damage, and managed the extraordinary feat of building a single new aircraft out of scraps taken from the three wrecks.

Still we managed to keep the U-boats submerged – and by now the submarine threat had receded markedly. In the first three months of 1944, some 3,500 merchant ships had crossed the North Atlantic in one direction or other, and only three had been sunk. But in that same period twenty-nine U-boats had been destroyed. Admiral Dönitz had lost. Johnnie Walker and our old Escort Group 2 had long since moved to protecting the fleets in the English Channel.

But Dönitz still had more than four hundred submarines; there was no question of leaving the convoys unescorted. So we circled endlessly above them, much of our time spent in locating stragglers, old freighters than had broken down or simply couldn't keep up with the convoy or had been hit or had got lost – and bringing them or at least their crews to safety.

As we approached St John's, Newfoundland, I laid my plans for a new consignment of birdseed. I had a week ashore, and I scurried from chandler to chandler looking for it, only to discover that the sole variety available was a very small grain, too small for the liking of budgerigars. Rather anxiously, I bought three kitbags-full.

*

Empire MacCabe returned to the Clyde. There was a signal waiting for the Captain, which he showed to me:

> Sub-Lieutenant Le Page of 836 Squadron is considerably overdue for operational leave, and should be sent immediately on indefinite home leave on your arrival in the UK. An immediate replacement will be sent to you. Le Page's promotion to Lieutenant (A) is also gazetted.

I was getting on still – but now I really had had enough of flying at sea.

When I got back to London, I set off with my bulging kitbags to find a lady and her son who had advertised in *Cage Birds Monthly*. She peered at the paltry seed in my bags, and said with the deepest regret that she could not possibly pay me £100 for a hundredweight of this stuff; she was doing herself down giving me even £64. 'Such a shame,' she said, 'and after you've been to such trouble bringing it over.'

Maybe, for all my accountancy skills, I was ripped off. I had £200, not the £300 I'd been expecting. But it was still a very considerable profit; I'd only paid sixpence a pound for the seed in Newfoundland, and I had my Navy pay. My pockets were full of money.

The war was receding from Britain. When I rejoined Gina and her family in Eltham, the fear was draining away from the town. The buzz-bombs and rockets were finished; the war in Europe had moved east and south, and the UK was swarming with American and Canadian servicemen: 'overpaid, oversexed and over here' as British servicemen grumbled jealously. Gina went each day to her job in Martin's Bank at Hanover Square in the West End of London, where one of her tasks was to go to their head office in the City, to collect cash – not by armoured security truck, but by taxi. One day, returning with her stash of loot, she was just climbing back into the taxi when three Canadians suddenly piled in beside her and commandeered the vehicle. She smiled demurely, saying nothing of what she was carrying, and they paid for the ride to Hanover Square.

Sometimes I was able to meet her as she finished work, and we could go out for the evening: there was a nightclub in a basement next to the bank. But I was uneasy; three weeks of kicking my heels was not only boring: it was making me anxious. The fighting was not done yet. Even if the FAA had less and less to do in the Atlantic, the Arctic convoys were still going. (John Godley would soon take command of an escort carrier squadron on one of the very last convoys in January 1945, the conditions as tough as ever.)

And the Pacific War was far from over. That's where Freddie Nottingham was. That's where Swordfish were still flying from carriers, and the agile Japanese fighters had been shooting down Swordfish since 1942 when half a dozen Stringbags had been caught in a corridor of barrage balloons and had been picked off, helpless…

No, I didn't want to sail again. I decided to make a pre-emptive strike, and went to the Admiralty. Once again, the desk officer was surprised: was I really bored with home leave so soon? Still, he had just the thing for me: the Observer Training School at Arbroath, where I had learned all my navigational skills. They needed (they claimed) yet another instructor. I'd be just the man. And I'd be back in Arbroath, pretty much where I'd started.

We had an old crock of a car, a little sit-up-and-beg Austin. At the end of October 1944, I loaded it and set off for the far north, with Gina to follow by train when I'd found somewhere to live.

An amiable Lieutenant Commander K.C. Grieve (RN) was running the so-called 'Reconnaissance School' at Arbroath. He'd created it himself, and he appointed me to his personal staff where, to my delight, I found Don Ridgway; he'd come there straight from 816 Squadron. He was teaching an orthodox course in all the navigation stuff we had learned ourselves nearly three years beforehand. I, meanwhile, was allowed to extemporise a course of lectures and exercises based on my experiences and what I could find in the library. But I was finding it increasingly hard to relate to what I was teaching, and I knew little about the Pacific. We were all just finding ways to pass the time.

Gina arrived. I had found us lodgings in a rather small bungalow in Arbroath town, the premises of Mrs Cousins. It was very cramped. Gina had to share the kitchen with Mrs Cousin who kept a careful and very economical eye on all our doings. I bought for Gina a small 'utility radio' (the only sort you could get). The next day, Mrs Cousins – having had a good prowl in our absence – appeared in the doorway of our sitting room.

'That's a bonny wee radio you've bought, Mr Le Page,' she said in her broad Angus accent. 'That'll be a shullin a week extra for the electric.'

Stunned, I at last said that I'd pay her whatever the Electricity Board told us it would cost to run if we left it on all day. When I asked, I was told it would probably be about a penny a week; we settled for a penny a day.

But Mrs Cousins was not going to drop her guard; every day she hovered around Gina, watching and remarking. As a young bride in a foreign land, and barely able to speak the language, Gina found it more and more wearing. Hot water and warmth were meanly rationed. There was just one source for both: our living room fire with a back-boiler behind it. Mrs Cousins believed that a single live coal at a time was sufficient to our purposes, and certainly no more than one bath a week. Those were the days when government propaganda was telling everyone to paint a black mark in their baths giving a depth of five inches of hot water. Our baths were three inches.

We had to move. I heard that another instructor – known as 'Wacky' Keppel – was leaving. I acted quickly, meeting his landlady to see if we could take over. But the rent (£4 a week) was above our budget. What to do? We went to Don Ridgway, newly married, and put a proposal to him – and we applied for joint tenancy.

The house was Abbey Lodge. Arbroath Abbey was an immense sandstone ruin on a hilltop dominating the town. It had been founded by King William the Lion in 1178, and there in 1320 Robert the Bruce had signed Scotland's Declaration of Independence. The lodge stood just outside the Abbey gates, very large and four-square. It was owned by a lady of aristocratic pretensions. In December 1944, the four of us moved in.

I led Gina, Don and his wife Margaret in through the front door: 'Bloody hell,' said Don. 'It's Buckingham Palace.'

Just inside the door there was a large iron cooking pot alleged to have belonged to the Bruce himself; we used it for our brollies and walking sticks. On the ground floor was a large drawing room with sofa and rugs, and starkly formal dining room containing a vast mahogany dining table with stiffly upright Victorian dining chairs but with armchairs at facing ends. On the walls were four huge etchings of stirring events: Nelson at Trafalgar, Wellington at Waterloo... On the end wall, a painted Cupid was on the wing, eternally poised to fire love's darts into whomsoever sat in the armchair at the head of the table. At the top of the grand staircase there were three large bedrooms, each with a small gas fire, and a vast and Arctic bathroom. There were huge cellars to accommodate all the housemaids and wine that we did not have.

Outside, there was a cluster of fruit trees in a large garden whose high stone wall overlooked a steep drop to the High Street and the shops.

We drew lots: Don and Margaret got the drawing room, Gina and I had to settle for Cupid and Wellington in the dining room, where the historic etchings recalled *The Return of the Lifeboat*, my father's inheritance from Guernsey. We really were getting on – so much so that one morning Gina came out of the kitchen to find a party of ladies being escorted up the grand staircase, their guide being under the impression that this was still the abbot's house.

So, through that hard winter we lived in chilly grandeur. Gina and Margaret shared the vast kitchen with its antique gas stove. The only dispute that I can recall was my fault: I pointed out that every other housewife in Arbroath holystoned her front doorstep to a righteous gleam each day. Margaret and Gina looked at me very coldly; our doorstep remained a disgrace to the town.

One day I caught a group of children up the fruit trees in the garden, scrumping apples. When I came out of the house they all swarmed over the garden wall and dropped the twelve feet down into the High Street – all except for one terrified girl whom they abandoned up a tree. I got her down and marched her inside, in front of Don as he sat in his big armchair like an examining magistrate. Putting on his very gravest expression, he began to tell her that she was a very naughty girl indeed at which point we realized that she was wetting her knickers over his carpet.

*

We were bored, we were frustrated; our lives were slipping away. What we were doing meant nothing. We did our best to amuse ourselves, and for me this meant amateur dramatics. I'd been keen at school: Christ's Hospital boys used to put on plays at epileptic hospitals and borstals. So, in Arbroath, I was one of those organizing a production of Ian Hay's *Housemaster*, a very light comedy.[3] I played the youthful lead opposite a very glamorous Wren officer called Olga (*plate 29*) .She had been a model before the war; a couple of months previous to our play, a very revealing photo of Olga had graced the cover of a gentleman's magazine. When we did the play at the air station, the mere sight of her brought the house down with wolf whistles. Soon afterwards, we had a rather more restrained success in the Arbroath 'toon hoos', with all the burghers and their ladies in the audience eating sweeties and reserving their applause and their laughter until they were sure that they were going to get a good evening's entertainment for their half-crowns.

What else to do? One night, two of my colleagues got drunk and hit upon a prank. The main railway line from Edinburgh and Dundee north to Aberdeen passed through the town; my colleagues went out and stole a couple of red lanterns from nearby roadworks, then waited by the line at some remote country spot. As a huge express train came snorting towards them, they waved their red lanterns at it like the Railway Children, and the driver saw and brought the great engine to a juddering emergency halt. Driver and footplateman jumped down from the cab and came running alongside the line, expecting to be told that a landslide had dragged the embankments into the sea. They found two FAA officers, still waving their lanterns.

'What is it? What's the matter?'

My friends beamed at them, and enquired in Shakespearean tones: 'What news?'

'Eh?'

'What news from London town?'

There was no news.

We were not at peace, and it began to show. I started to get into trouble.

Every weekday, Don and I set off for the air station to give the new recruits the benefit of our vast experience of the sea war fought from the air. By now I had the distinct impression that nobody knew quite what the Reconnaissance School was supposed to be doing, apart from keeping half-a-dozen pilots and observers like Don and me off the streets after completing two operational tours.

From time to time, Lieutenant Commander Grieve would send me off on a refresher course. One of these concerned 'Combined Operations', which meant a week working with Army and RAF staff. It was interesting in its way, but it all related to the past, a past fought in very different conditions to the present. We learned, for example, how to coordinate gunfire from British and American forces onto shore targets, as though we were preparing to invade Normandy all over again. Nobody mentioned the very different scenario in the Far East, or the island-hopping assaults moving across the Pacific towards Japan.

At the end of the course there was a discussion session. We had been broken up into mixed groups, and at the end my group appointed me as spokesman. I stated, much too bluntly, my opinion of retrospective tacticians. When I returned to Arbroath, Grieve sent for me. He had had a letter of complaint from the course organizers concerning the lack of respect I had shown; I was, after all, merely a young RNVR lieutenant. His rebuke was mild, but I knew that I was marked.

I put my best energies into my lectures, reading up everything I could. I tried hard to make them relate to the Pacific war, which by now was the only thing that mattered to the Navy. One of my best performances was on the Battle of Midway – the great naval battle in which the American and Japanese fleets never saw each other, but slugged it out with carrier-borne aircraft over a distance of more than a hundred miles. I put my heart into teaching. I liked it; I was good at it. I was building a reputation…

But I was getting another reputation too: for shooting my mouth off.

We were invited out to dinner from time to time by one of the local landowners, a grand but entertaining lady: The Honourable Mrs Lindsay Carnegie. She had taken a liking to us because somehow I always managed to make her laugh. We happened to be there with some senior naval officers and one or two of her neighbouring landowners the evening that the general election results started to come through on the radio. As the extent of Attlee and the Labour Party's victory became increasingly obvious, the landowners' faces grew longer and longer; their world was coming to an end. I couldn't resist it: I said, rather loudly and forcefully, what a very fine thing it was, what a victory for democracy... At which one very senior officer took me into a corner and told me sternly that as a young and junior officer I had no business expressing such opinions in front of our hostess.

If I had been to Dartmouth Naval college – if only I had been a regular Navy man, and not a jumped-up window cleaner's son from South London – I would of course have known better manners. I should never have presumed so far. I had got on, but at this rate I would not be going much further.

Mrs Carnegie didn't care. She was as amused as I was by the funereal effect the election news was having on her fellow landowners. She was a far-from-pompous person. One evening, when we had invited her to dinner at Abbey Lodge, she arrived in one of her home farm lorries, driven by her chauffeur; it pretty much blocked the narrow street. She explained that it contained all that was left of her petrol ration for the month. Her chauffeur had to help her climb down from the cab, amid many giggles as she disentangled the skirt of her dress.

I did very little flying now, and it was all land-based and by day. We had no Swordfish any more at Arbroath; I had to get used to a new aircraft, the Fairey Barracuda, which in common with almost all aircrew I greatly disliked. It was so cluttered, so inelegant, so ugly, that when the first Barracuda landed on the USS *Saratoga* a USN lieutenant reportedly said, 'Jesus Christ! The Limeys'll be building airplanes next.'

The FAA pilot Terence Horsley, in his 1944 propaganda book on the service, attempted to be positive about the Barracuda. It was very easy to fly, he claimed. I had my copy of his little book by then, and tried my best to be persuaded when he wrote that it was a clever design with many advantages, that it really was very safe in deck landings. Moreover, he asserted that it was 'remarkably tractable for so heavy a machine at low speeds', although 'one might feel a sense of alarm to watch it coming down with its nose held high and its tail well down, until one realizes how safe it is at this attitude...'

Had Horsley ever flown one? It might have been safe in landing-on, but a string of mysterious accidents and uncontrollable spins (something a Swordfish was quite incapable of) had made the Barracuda feared by aircrews. The last flight that John Godley ever made was in a Barracuda. He was back at HMS Daedalus, Lee-on-Solent, doing a conversion course on monoplanes. One day he noticed a Barracuda coming in over the airfield – the pilot, like himself, with long hours of Swordfish experience – and John watched it suddenly, inexplicably and fatally spin out of control into the ground in front of his eyes. A few weeks later, back in charge of his squadron at Crimond (near Aberdeen), John took up his own Barracuda and was nearing the airfield for landing when a pipe in the cockpit cracked and his face was suddenly covered in a fine spray of hydraulic fluid, toxic and suffocating. He just managed to land before passing out, and he never piloted an aircraft again.

It turned out that this was one of the causes of the frequent crashes. I at least didn't have to pilot the things. The Barracuda had just a few items in its favour: it was a novelty to fly in an enclosed cockpit, and at speeds dizzily in excess of the Swordfish's usual 85 knots. But I hated it; I didn't trust it; I feared it. I no longer wanted to fly at all. Like John, I was thoroughly 'twitched'.

After several months of this – lecturing on anything we could think of, and flying as little as we could contrive – Lieutenant Commander Grieve decided that he'd best make sure we were all keeping our hands in, and he organized an airborne navigation competition in our bloody Barracudas. Now, there was something that I could do! That was what I was good at, that was where I shone. I determined that once again I would do it faultlessly, as in every competition, as in my chemistry final at Christ's Hospital... I won, of course. But on the last leg of the navigation, I realized that I had in fact made an error, and I added in a sly correction. I cheated. It was my final triumph in the FAA.

At home shortly afterwards, I was coming out of the kitchen to meet Gina, when at that moment we heard on the radio the news of the dropping of the first atomic bomb. We knew at once that it meant the end of war. Gina and I 'stared at each other with a wild surmise'[4] at the foot of the Abbey Lodge staircase – then turned back into the kitchen to listen greedily to the bulletin.

*

I was disintegrating; I could feel it – in fact it was becoming painfully obvious. I had become explosive of temper and had given several senior officers a piece of my mind. I was given to crying uncontrollably for no reason at all. I needed to get out fast – but to what? Back to Mr L. I. Grant at Messrs Barton & Mayhew, Chartered Accountants, of St Botolph's, Bishopsgate? Was my past my future? I cried some more...

In my car, I knocked an old lady down in an Arbroath street. It was her fault, absolutely, she stepped out from the pavement, she wasn't looking where she was going... Thankfully, she was not much hurt. But it took Ernie Myles and his influence in Arbroath society to still the unkind rumours about me.

What to do?

On VJ night I went drinking in the wardroom of the airbase with a visiting friend: Dave Wormald, my pilot from 836 Squadron.

'What are you going to do now, Dave?'

'I'm going back to Oxford. Why don't you come?'

'Would they have me?'

'Why don't you try?'

I hitched a flight down to RAF Culham the next week, and went into Oxford feeling like Jude the Obscure. But before the war I had audited the accounts of Queen's College, and I knew their Bursar well.

'I've only got basic Matriculation,' I told him, 'five credits at School Certificate. Is it worth applying?'

'Not to us. We're going to be full up with all the people who had started degree courses before the outbreak, and will be coming back to finish them. But why don't you try Keble? They've been the Ministry of Ag & Fish all through the war. They've got no students at all.'

I walked through the Turl and along Parks Road to the red-brick fortress of Keble College, and was told that I could see the Dean at teatime. He was a shrivelled, drip-nosed little man called Leonard Rice-Oxley, but he gave me a cup of tea.

'I'll work very hard!' I pleaded.

'And what would you want to read?'

'English literature. I've always wanted to.'

'You have done some Latin, I suppose?'

'Oh, yes.'

'And where did you go to school?'

'Christ's Hospital.'

'Ah, yes. Well, I think that will be all right.'

I could hardly believe it: me – at Oxford! I walked on air.

There were two problems. Firstly: did I have the money to support Gina and myself at Oxford for three years? Well, I had my war gratuity, about £400. And I had several hundred pounds from smuggling birdseed. But then: how was I going to get out of the FAA by October?

I hitched another flight back to Arbroath and broke the news to Gina.

'My Uncle Wyndham,' she said, 'thinks you're a fool not to stay in the Navy. You're an officer, a lieutenant and only twenty-four. Why throw it all away?'

But I shook my head.

'It's impossible. You know me: I could barely stand the bullshit in wartime, let alone now in the peace. Anyway, they wouldn't have me. I'm ripe for a court martial as it is.'

Which was only too true. Rather hurriedly, I went to see a friendly Surgeon-Commander, and told him all the symptoms: luckily I had an operational record that made them plausible.

'You want out, I suppose?'

'As soon as I can.'

He only gave me the time to pack a bag before putting me into a naval transport to the Royal Naval Psychiatric hospital at Kingseat, near Aberdeen. It was a vast old stately home, converted into a mental hospital. A Petty Officer opened a grille at the entrance, unlocked the front door to let me in, then shut and bolted it behind me, cackling:

'You're in now. You won't get out again!'

'Why's that?' I felt a ghastly creeping chill.

'Captain only gets to keep his rank as long as he can muster the right number of patients. Nobody gets out!'

I crept through the hospital, shocked: I was surrounded by profoundly disturbed naval officers. Some were having electro-convulsive therapy – ECT. Others, like me, were having drug-induced deep sleep therapy, a thoroughly dangerous procedure involving an insulin-induced coma, which would supposedly give the brain a chance to re-wire itself, if the insulin overdose didn't kill you first. Some patients talked endlessly, compulsively, about themselves. Others remained absolutely silent. Four of us played poker or liar dice – all day, every day. One of the four was a trawler skipper who had twice had his ship blown apart by mines. He would get out of the bed opposite me each morning and stare out of the window.

'What's it like, Dickie?'

'Thick fog. Won't get into Suez today.'

His neighbour in the next bed was a submariner, the only regular Navy officer in the ward and filled with contempt for the 'Wavy Navy' RNVR. In the middle of the night, he would get out of bed and walk round ringing every bell push he could see, then try to line everybody up – nurses and all – for inspection.

'Look at your hands, Nurse Brown: they're filthy!'

'Now, now, Lieutenant Cook, it's back to your bed, please, and no more nonsense tonight.'

'Yes, come on, Cookie, we all want to get some sleep.'

'Sleep? That's all you bloody lot think about. What about the efficiency of the Service?'

'Sod the Service, Cookie – go to sleep!'

He would stamp back to his bed muttering: 'Wavy bloody navy. Undisciplined bloody rubbish.'

To which we would reply with a softly crooned lullaby: *There's a balls-up on the flight deck, and the Wavy Navy done it…*

Meanwhile, in Arbroath, Gina was surprised at the amount of sympathy she was getting.

'You poor dear. It must have been hell for you.'

'Oh,' she would murmur, worried, 'I don't know that he's that bad.'

'Oh yes,' her friends assured her. 'George said he punched Commander Grieve in the face and had to be taken away in a straitjacket.'

Rumour sped around the air station, among my friends and acquaintance in the town, and even reaching my sisters in London.

But just two weeks later, I reappeared in Arbroath. I had threatened to start throwing the furniture around, and they had let me out. I was discharged, with no stain on my character.

Gina and I loaded up our decrepit old Austin with all our valuables for the long drive south. I went for a last piss-up with the boys from the air station, driving out in two car-loads. As we approached the gate, I tooted BULLSHIT in Morse on my horn. The Duty Quartermaster stopped me.

'Was that you tooting?'

'No, Chief – car behind.'

We drove out.

To the car behind: 'Was that you tooting?'

'Of course not, Chief – fellow in front.'

It was quite a party. As we drove back at midnight along a deserted road in the crisp moonlight, the white line ahead of me weaved (or wove) around my headlights. Thus I took my leave of the Fleet Air Arm (*plate 30*).

*

Some weeks later, I drove alone from London to Oxford, through the beech woods of the Chilterns in beautiful Indian summer sunshine. I had to spend my first term living in college before Gina could join me. I was given a set of rooms on the ground floor adjoining the clock tower; beneath the clock were the only six baths in the college. I had a sitting room, and a tiny bedroom, and a scout, Mr Collett, to clean up for me and bring me buckets of coal for the fire. In the morning, he would examine the cigarette butts in the ashtray: 'You've 'ad women in 'ere.'

Dave Wormald was at Jesus, finishing his degree in modern languages. My close companions at Keble were an Australian bomber pilot – now studying Greek – and a New Zealand Coastal Command pilot who was reading forestry. We had been used to generous service rations, not the sort of food civilians had had to survive on, and now the college had our ration books. On our first day, we had gone to lunch in hall, decorously served by the scouts: bread, water, and one half of a tomato each, thinly sliced upon a plate.

'Is that it?'

'That's all there is, sir.'

We went hurriedly round the shops: I bought a Valor oil stove, a frying pan, and some sort of ersatz frying oil, and we begged and bullied at a grocer's until we came away with milk powder and some dried eggs. I made revolting 'scrambled eggs' and we sat about on the floor of my room devouring it.

We would survive.

Whether I would survive Oxford itself was another matter. In the coming months, there were times when it got me down badly. Although I was also being taught by the outstanding medievalists C.S. Lewis, Nevill Coghill and J.R.R. Tolkien (never mind the hobbits; he was a fine scholar), still the majority of the dons – men like Leonard Rice-Oxley, who had let me in – were, to my bad-tempered and intolerant state of mind, just a waste of time as teachers.[5] We were far from being the licentious soldiery let loose on Oxford in 1919; we had lost five years of our lives and were hurrying to catch up. We had little interest in Rice-Oxley's tales of college derring-do, of Freshers' Blinds at which the Second and Third Year men bought the First Years all the beer they could drink, or the Bumps Suppers after which they burned a boat in the quad. We had seen quite enough of burning boats.

So I began another poem:

Spleen

Books, books, books – I'm sick of 'em,
Dons as well – take your pick of 'em.
Nothing but pious old women, the best of 'em,
Idle self-satisfied spivs, the rest of 'em.

Oxford's a cabbage without roots,
Putting out sickly pale-green shoots
Before it dies; North Oxford stinks
Of smug complacency and soft drinks.

Keble I hate most of all –
The barbed wire top to its prison wall,
Its dreary dons and deadly monotony,
Its hideous chapel, a brick-buttressed blot-on-the

Landscape. God, I must take a train,
Get away from this inland plain,
From staring cows and staring people
Where nothing's higher than St Mary's steeple.

Scholarship is not my line.
Keep its thin beer: give me the whine
Of a mountain wind on an April morning,
Or the North Atlantic, with day dawning
Over a storm-wracked, fretting, heaving
Mass of oceans…

I had not yet left the sea or the sea-air behind. For some long time at Oxford, because clothing was in such short supply, I still wore my uniform of a naval lieutenant. I had a 20 per cent disability pension as a war-traumatized psychoneurotic. I had spinal injuries as a result of harsh deck landings that kept me in pain for the rest of my life.

Nothing had changed. Everything had changed.

Notes

1. The speed of US shipbuilding was astonishing. One wartime freighter was built from keel-laying to hull launch in seven days.
2. *Empire MacCabe* was built by Swan Hunter on the Clyde and launched in December 1943. At 9,249 tons displacement, she was 462 feet long. She was operated by British Petroleum.
3. John Hay Beith ('Ian Hay') was a soldier who made a second career as a dramatist. He wrote several well known plays and screenplays including *Housemaster*, remembered for its line: 'What do you mean, funny? Funny-peculiar or funny ha-ha?'
4. From John Keats' sonnet *On First Looking into Chapman's Homer*.
5. Robert's academic autobiography, *Ivory Towers* (1998), continues to be hard on Leonard Rice-Oxley, but also mentions that the tutor asked Robert's advice about getting married, before wedding 'a very nice large dignified lady twice his size who shepherded him around the British Restaurant like a shunting engine with a truck.'

Afterword

by

Jonathan Falla

In 1945, everyone was in a hurry to put the war behind them and move on.

Towards the Swordfish aircraft, there was little gratitude from the authorities. The Swordfish was possibly the only machine to be in service from the very outset of the war until the very end. Never mind the new designs and developments: although the last Stringbag was delivered from the factory in August 1944, they continued to serve long afterwards. No. 836, the Mac-ship squadron, was the last Swordfish unit, and was finally disbanded on 21 May 1945, but a concluding operational mission was flown a month later. Swordfish were still being used as FAA trainers in the summer of 1946.

But with the end of the war, most of the aircraft were scrapped. Not just scrapped, in fact, but utterly destroyed: pilots brought them all to an airfield near Manchester, where they were incinerated. One 836 Squadron pilot – Stanley Brand – described splashing over the paraffin and setting fire to his own aircraft, remarking that it felt like taking a faithful old dog to the vet to be put down.[1]

No. 816 Squadron had ceased to exist in Britain, but was reconstituted as part of the Royal Australian Air Force, using the same motto – 'Imitate the Action of the Tiger' – and the same badge of a tiger's snarling face, but with the addition of a boomerang and a stone axe crossed underneath, a touch of the airworthy but primitive that would have rather suited Swordfish.

The aircrew went their ways and looked to make new lives and careers, sometimes in institutions almost as grand as the Royal Navy: Brian Bennett went into the Bank of England; Bill Laing (having been a medical student before the war) entered the church; Don Ridgway became a director of ASDA. But not a few of them roamed the old Empire, perhaps hoping to maintain the strange self-reliant freedoms of flying: John Beresford went to South Africa; Dave Wormald became a tea planter in India and then a farmer in Cornwall. While some made the most of the discipline and determination they had learned, others found it less easy. Ken Horsfield had something to do with importing cars into central Africa, but took to the bottle and died in his fifties. Others just could not settle. John Godley had, like Robert, been officially grounded by a surgeon-commander as no longer mentally fit to fly. He wandered the world, got through two marriages and pursued a somewhat half-hearted career as an author. He produced, amongst other things, two books on nature spotting. But his best-remembered publication, the most vivid and immediate, was his Swordfish book: *Bring Back My Stringbag*.

Luck – or at least chance – continued to play a considerable part in Robert's life. The birdseed money helped put him through Oxford. After taking his degree, with post-graduate work at Birmingham, he went in 1950 to Jamaica (where 816 Squadron had originally been formed) as one of the early faculty at the new University of the West Indies. There he taught Anglo-Saxon poetry to West Indian students; he found that, often coming from impoverished rural backgrounds, they understood the earthy, life-threatening concerns of Anglo-Saxon life rather better than did students from the English middle classes.

But in Jamaica his interest in language was steered in very new directions, in part by a newspaper competition: the *Jamaica Gleaner* offered a prize for the best collection of interesting vernacular, and Robert inherited the stack of entries. They included items such as: 'Gonorrhoea – gentlemen's complaint.'

As a result of this, he began work with the American linguist Fred Cassidy on a *Dictionary of Jamaican English*, which was published by Cambridge University Press and remains a standard authority today.

He moved to a Chair in English at the University of Malaya in 1960, until the opening of a new Department of Language at York University in 1964 with Robert as professor. Apart from forays to the United States, Singapore and Hong Kong, he remained at York for the rest of his career. When he finally retired in 1988, he was recognized as one of the world's foremost experts in multi-cultural sociolinguistics. He had certainly got on.

But the FAA never left him – certainly not that spinal injury from deck landings, which for the rest of his life sent him from doctor to doctor, therapy to therapy, seeking a cure. I watched him as a frail, elderly man near to tears, saying: 'No more pain. I've had enough of pain.'

Nor did it ever quite leave him in his attitudes and manner, about which he was resolutely honest. He always remained a little guarded with Germans that he met (although becoming proficient in the language). He also found it difficult to stop being an officer. In his own academic autobiography,[2] he reprinted in full an appraisal of him written by Jamaican students at the time of his leaving the Caribbean. The students were not altogether kind: some people (they said) called Le Page a bohemian, a cynic and a snob. Others found him likeable if a little distant: 'A less reserved manner … could not have lessened his popularity.' He himself commented:

> It is clear from their verdict that I could have done better if I had tried. I wish very much in retrospect that I had, but obviously I had found it difficult to throw off the inhibitions of my naval training.

This changed. At York, he threw himself not only into academic research and teaching, but also into the affairs and well-being of his students, becoming provost of a college, patron to young people who were also trying to find their way into adulthood. As his York motto had it: The tone was low, but the quality was high.

For the rest of his life, there was at times a distracted and introspective quality to Robert, even when he was being convivial. In the group photograph taken at the 1991 reunion of 816 Squadron (there were fourteen of the officer aircrew present), Robert stands in the back row. He is the only one not smiling at the camera, but is thinking of something else, distantly.

Notes

1. *Achtung! Swordfish!* by Stanley Brand (2005).
2. *Ivory Towers: Memoirs of a Pidgin Fancier* (1998).

Index